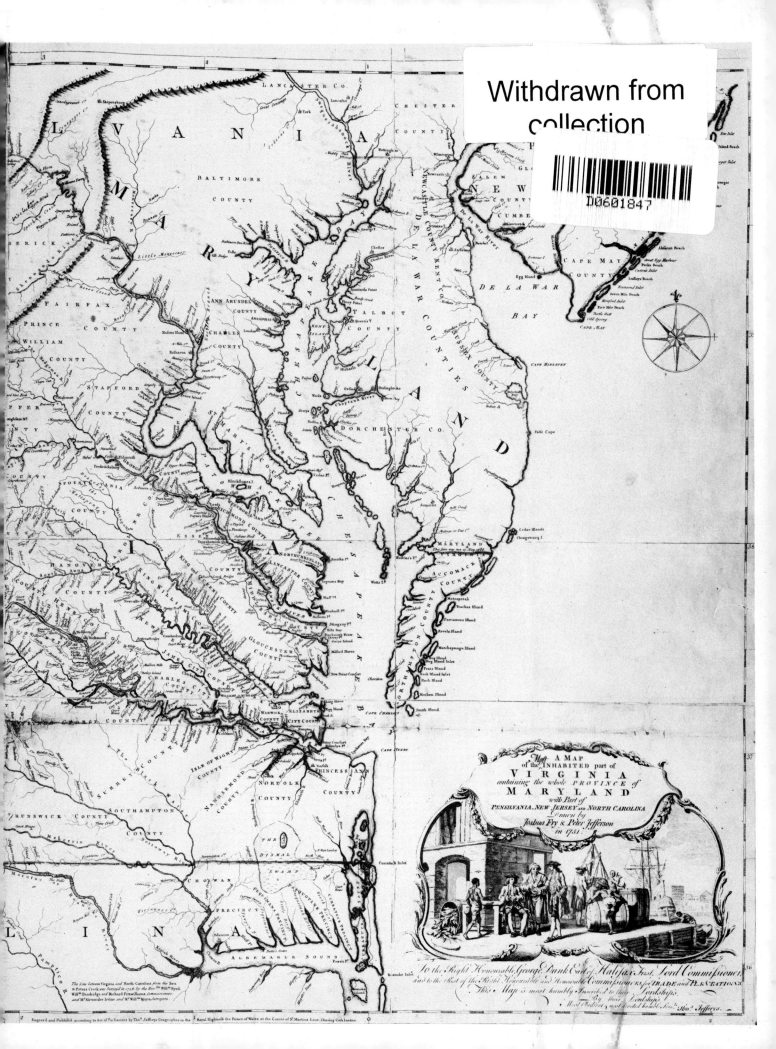

A MAP
of the INHABITED part of
VIRGINIA
containing the whole PROVINCE of
MARYLAND
with Part of
PENSILVANIA, NEW JERSEY AND NORTH CAROLINA
Drawn by
Joshua Fry & Peter Jefferson
in 1751

To the Right Honourable, George, Dunk Earl of Halifax, First, Lord Commissioner, and to the Rest of the Right Honourable and Honourable Commissioners, for TRADE and PLANTATIONS. This Map is most humbly Inscribed to their Lordships. By their Lordships. Most Obedient, & most devoted humble Serv.t Tho.s Jefferys.

Mr. Jefferson Architect

Mr. Jefferson Architect

Desmond Guinness & Julius Trousdale Sadler, Jr.

A STUDIO BOOK · THE VIKING PRESS · NEW YORK

Design by Christopher Holme

Copyright © 1973 by The Viking Press, Inc.
All rights reserved
First published in 1973 by The Viking Press, Inc.
625 Madison Avenue, New York, N.Y. 10022
Published simultaneously in Canada by
The Macmillan Company of Canada Limited
SBN 670-49261-2
Second Printing July 1974
Library of Congress catalog card number: 72-12057
Printed in U.S.A.

CONTENTS

This book is dedicated to
Patrick and Marina Guinness
and
Jason and Garrett Sadler

INTRODUCTION

Thomas Jefferson's architectural achievement is one of the more remarkable facets of that amazing genius, although it is only natural that it should have been obscured by his better-known accomplishments. Yet if he had never entered politics, become President of the United States, or drafted the Declaration of Independence that made history in Philadelphia on July 4, 1776, he might be remembered to this day as the first truly American architect. He was no slavish copyist, although much of his inspiration came from the architectural pattern books that were current in his day, and from the buildings that he saw and admired in Europe. Nonetheless, with its simple clear-cut lines and understated ornament, his architecture seems peculiarly at home in the brilliant Virginia sun.

Jefferson spent five years, from 1784 to 1789, as Minister and Ambassador in Paris, besides which he traveled extensively in France and England, looking at buildings and gardens, and even penetrated into Italy as far as Milan. He approved of the English informal garden that had by then shaken off the formal French or Dutch straitjacket. English architecture, on the other hand, he found "the most wretched style I ever saw." He admired the buildings of his day in France, but only up to a point: purity of line was in keeping with the puritan in him; carvings, statues, and almost all supplementary exterior ornament are forgotten in his work. Monticello is a distillation of all that he admired most in Europe—the garden English, the scale French, and the simplicity of line Italian.

Thomas Jefferson was born in 1743 at Shadwell, not far from the foot of the hill on which Monticello now stands. He was the eldest son of Peter Jefferson and Mary Randolph. Peter Jefferson had been granted 1000 acres of rich land here in 1735, stretching from the banks of the Rivanna River to the foothills of

The Bodleian Plate: "The only public buildings worthy of mention are the capitol, the palace, the college . . . all of them in Williamsburg." After remodeling in order to present a more impressive face to the newly important Duke of Gloucester Street, ". . . the capitol is a light and airy structure with a portico in front of two orders. . . . The Palace is not handsome without, but is spacious and commodious within. . . ." Patrick Henry and Thomas Jefferson occupied the palace as the first two Governors of the Commonwealth. "The college and hospital are rude misshapen piles. . . ."

This copperplate engraving, now in the Courthouse museum, Williamsburg, and formerly in the Bodleian Library, Oxford, represents the principal buildings of Williamsburg as they were in the mid-eighteenth century.

8

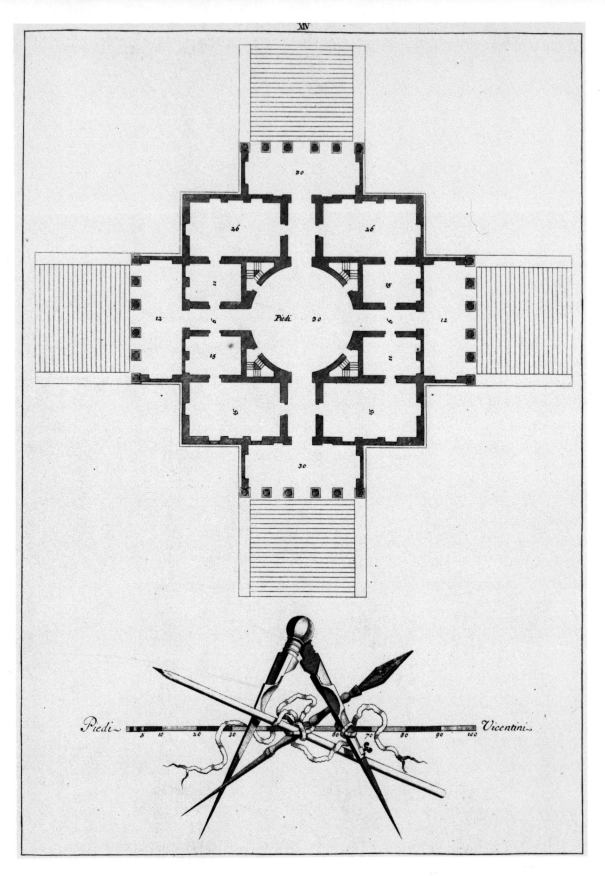

The Villa Rotunda: Plate XIV from *The Architecture of A. Palladio* . . . "Revis'd, Design'd, and Publish'd by Giacomo Leoni. . . ." Second Edition, London, 1721.

The Villa Rotunda: Plate XV from Leoni's Second Edition. Jefferson's interest in Palladian architecture was established during his early years at the College of William and Mary.

Gravé sous la conduite de B. Picart en 1715.

The Maison Carrée: Thomas Jefferson derived his original conception for the Capitol at Richmond from his copy of Leoni's *Palladio*.

The Pantheon: Much of the original kinship between Jefferson's design for the interior of the Rotunda at the University of Virginia and the Pantheon was lost in Stanford White's reconstruction of the building.

the Blue Ridge. He was a surveyor, and with Joshua Fry published in 1751 the second Map of Virginia.* Mary Randolph came from one of the best families in Virginia, and her family connections stood him in good stead.

His birthplace, Shadwell, was a very simple frame house, and Tuckahoe Plantation, where he lived between the ages of two and nine, was also largely a frame country house. Jefferson was first exposed to "real" architecture when he went to study at the College of William and Mary at Williamsburg. The College buildings he considered "rude, misshapen piles which, but they have roofs,

* Only three copies of this 1751 map have survived; one is at the University of Virginia, one at the New York Public Library, and one has recently come to light in the library of the Duke of Northumberland at Alnwick Castle, Alnwick, England.

Brandon: For his friend Nathaniel Harrison, owner of Brandon, Jefferson is said to have designed the central section and raised the two existing wings, thus creating a five-part composition in the Palladian manner for this house on the lower James.

Tuckahoe Plantation: The home of Colonel William
Randolph. As executor of this estate, Peter Jefferson
moved here when his son Thomas was two. The H-
plan of the house is unusual for the period and must
have appealed to Jefferson; one of his studies (*ca.* 1779)
for remodeling the Colonial Governor's Palace at Williamsburg shows a second mass equal to that of the main
building, connected to it by the crossbar of the ballroom
wing.

The house, the school building, and the plantation
street still remain, undisturbed, as Jefferson knew
them. Only now is their serenity threatened by a proposed limited-access highway which may shortly slash
across the plantation within a thousand feet of the house.

would be taken for brick kilns" and his comments on the Governor's Palace, where he was a regular visitor, were equally scathing. Jefferson is said to have purchased his first architectural pattern book from a cabinetmaker at the College gate. His early classical education at Tuckahoe, and his love of books and reading, gave him an excellent eye for architecture, which became one of his ruling passions.

During these years of study Jefferson developed an omnivorous taste for every aspect of learning that remained with him for the rest of his life. He was a considerable linguist, as well as a philosopher and a mathematician. He was an avid reader and amassed three libraries during the course of his long life. He was admitted to the bar in 1767 and returned to Shadwell to help his mother, now widowed, with the management of the family property. His reputation for integrity and hard work assured him a successful legal practice, and it was not long before the idea came to him of designing a new house for himself—a project which was to occupy him, as time and money allowed, for much of the remainder of his life.

THE EARLY MONTICELLO

All my wishes end, where I hope my days
will end, at Monticello

—Thomas Jefferson, 1787

As a young man, Jefferson was wont to set out from Shadwell in the cool of a long summer evening, after a hard day's work, cross the river, and there ascend the 800-foot hill that belonged to him. The view was, and still is, supreme. His decision to build on its summit was a departure from the usual custom of building beside a river, which could be used for transport, or on the flat land of the plain for convenience. "How sublime," he wrote many years later to Maria Cosway, "to look down into the workhouse of nature, to see her clouds, hail, snow, thunder all fabricated at our feet and the glorious sun when rising as if out of a distant water, just gilding the tops of the mountains. . . ."

In 1770 Shadwell and his precious books and papers were burned; very little was saved apart from his manuscript *Garden Book* and his fiddle. He now had every reason to hasten the work on Monticello, his "little mountain," and turn his dream into reality. The top of the mountain had already been leveled in 1768; he had paid in kind with 180 bushels of wheat and 24 of Indian corn for this operation, and already his kilns were at work making brick.

His plan was to make a broad terrace on the mountaintop, framed with twin promenades, beneath which could be concealed extensive out-offices, terminating in pavilions. In this way there would be nothing to interrupt the views from the house, and the comings and goings of the servants could pass unheeded. Work commenced in 1769, and was to continue in one way or another, from time to time, for forty years. "Architecture is my delight, and putting up and pulling down one of my favorite amusements." In view of this passion, and of the many alterations and improvements that he made over the years, to say nothing of financial and political crises, it is remarkable that Monticello should present such a balanced and integrated façade to the world today.

To start with, he finished the south pavilion and made it habitable by Christmas, 1770. "I have here but one room," he writes, "which, like the cobbler's, serves me for parlor, for kitchen, and hall. I may add for bedchamber and study too." The proportions of this little parlor are perfection itself, a startling achievement for the first building designed by a man of twenty-five. It is known as the Honeymoon.Cottage. It has always been supposed that Jefferson brought his bride of two weeks here in January 1772, coming the last several miles on horseback through a snowfall that had halted the carriage. Recently, during the course of repair work on this pavilion, foundations of an earlier structure have come to light, and it is now thought that the twin pavilions may have been rebuilt by Jefferson at a later date.

Jefferson's bride was a widow of twenty-three, Martha Wayles Skelton, and the marriage proved to be a happy one, although only two of their six children lived to maturity. The Marquis de Chastellux writes of a visit to Monticello in 1782:

> This house, of which Mr. Jefferson was the architect, and often the builder, is constructed in an Italian style, and is quite tasteful, although not however without some faults; it consists of a large square pavilion, into which one enters through two porticos ornamented with columns. The ground floor consists chiefly of a large and lofty *salon*, or drawing room, which is to be decorated entirely in the antique style; above the *salon* is a library of the same form; two small wings, with only a ground floor and attic, are joined to this pavilion, and are intended to communicate with the kitchen, offices, etc. which will form on either side a kind of basement topped by a terrace. My object in giving these details is not to describe the house, but to prove that it resembles none of the others seen in this country; so that it may be said that Mr. Jefferson is the first American who has consulted the Fine Arts to know how he should shelter himself from the weather. But it is with him alone that I should concern myself.
>
> Let me then describe to you a man, not yet forty, tall, with a mild and pleasing countenance, but whose mind and attainments could serve

in lieu of all outward graces. . . . A gentle and amiable wife, charming children whose education is his special care, a house to embellish, extensive estates to improve, the arts and sciences to cultivate—these are what remain to Mr. Jefferson, after having played a distinguished role on the stage of the New World, and what he has preferred to the honorable commission of Minister Plenipotentiary in Europe.

Shortly after this letter was written, Mrs. Jefferson died, in the tenth year of their marriage; Jefferson remained single for the rest of his life, and no longer avoided further public service.

Another French traveler has put his impressions of a visit to Monticello

Monticello, the south pavilion: This building is known as the Honeymoon Cottage; here Jefferson moved after Shadwell was burned, and here he brought his bride on a bitter night in 1772.

OVERLEAF: Monticello, 1771: Jefferson's drawing of the final elevation of the early version of Monticello. The octagonal ends, which were built, are not shown here, and the upper portico which appears in the drawing was apparently not completed.

down on paper for posterity. The Duc de la Rochefoucauld writes, in June of 1796:

In private life Mr. Jefferson displays a mild, easy and obliging temper, though he is somewhat cold and reserved. His conversation is of the most agreeable kind, and he possesses a stock of information not inferior to that of any other man. In Europe he would hold a distinguished rank among men of letters, and as such he has already appeared there. At present he is employed with activity and perseverance in the management of his farms and buildings; and he orders, directs and pursues in the minutest details every branch of business relative to them. I found him in the midst of the harvest, from which the scorching heat of the sun does not prevent his attendance. His negroes are nourished, clothed, and treated as well as white servants could be. As he cannot expect any assistance from the two small neighboring towns, every article is made on his farm: his negroes are cabinetmakers, carpenters, masons, bricklayers, smiths, etc. The children he employs in a small nail factory, which yields already a considerable profit. The young and old negresses spin for the clothing of the rest. He animates them by rewards and distinctions; in fine, his superior mind directs the management of his domestic concerns with the same abilities, activity and regularity which he evinced in the conduct of public affairs, and which he is calculated to display in every situation of life. In the superintendence of his household he is assisted by his two daughters, Mrs. Randolph and Miss Maria, who are handsome, modest, and amiable women. They have been educated in France. . . .

Mr. Randolph is proprietor of a considerable plantation, contiguous to that of Mr. Jefferson's. He constantly spends the summer with him, and, from the affection he bears him, he seems to be his son rather than his son-in-law. Miss Maria constantly resides with her father, but as she is seventeen years old, and is remarkably handsome, she will, doubtless, soon find that there are duties which it is still sweeter to perform than those of a daughter. Mr. Jefferson's philosophic turn of mind, his love of study, his excellent library, which supplies him with the means of satisfying it, and his friends, will undoubtedly help him to endure this loss, which, moreover, is not likely to become an absolute privation; as the second son-in-law of Mr. Jefferson may, like Mr. Randolph, reside in the vicinty of Monticello, and, if he be worthy of Miss Maria, will not be able to find any company more desirable than that of Mr. Jefferson. . . .

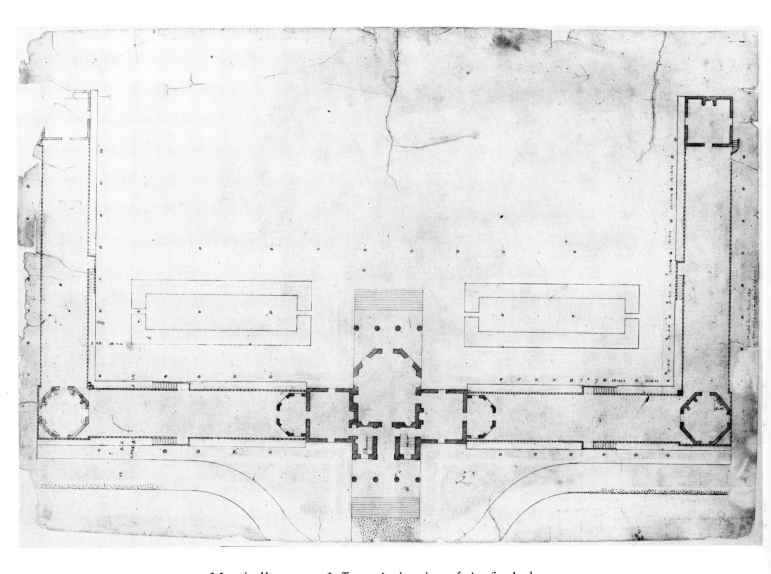

Monticello, 1771: Jefferson's drawing of the final plan for the early version of Monticello. The octagonal garden houses at the corners were not built.

Jefferson planned various decorative outbuildings to embellish the landscape. There was to be "a Chinese or Grecian temple, with an Aeolian harp humming mournfully with each whisper of the wind"—like the banshee. He planned a family graveyard on the property in 1771. In his Account Book for that year he writes: ". . . choose out for a burying place some unfrequented vale in the park, where is, 'no sound to break the stillness but a brook, that bubbling winds among the weeds; no mark of any human shape that had been there, unless the skeleton of some poor wretch, who sought that place out to despair and die in'.

Let it be among antient and venerable oaks; intersperse some gloomy evergreens . . . in the center of it erect a small Gothic temple of antique appearance. appropriate one half to the use of my own family, the other to strangers, servants, etc. erect pedestals with urns, etc., and proper inscriptions. the passage between the walls [*i.e.,* the entrance] 4 f wide. on the grave of a favorite and faithful servant might be a pyramid . . . in the middle of the temple an altar . . . very little light, perhaps none at all, save only the feeble ray of an half extinguished lamp." Everything but a hermit poring over a yellowing parchment! Jefferson writes of Greek, Gothic, and Chinese structures, and traces the garden temple in Gibbs's *Book of Architecture*. He envisaged classical towers with superimposed orders to serve as points of interest in the landscape seen from Monticello. He designed a pigeon house, with Tuscan columns and a stepped roof surmounted by an urn, and even a medieval tower with battlements and receding storeys. At one time he considered building octagonal temples at the corners of Monticello, a fanciful scheme, out of keeping with the rural simplicity of the house, which he rightly abandoned. His landscape follies remained on paper, and the house remained the focal point of a working plantation—indeed, when asked his occupation, Jefferson would always describe himself as a farmer.

The first plan for the house was taken from Morris's *Select Architecture*, but the elevation was derived from Palladio. The house had a two-storey portico flanked by slightly lower wings, of a type that is often seen in the Veneto. After the foundations were laid he elaborated slightly on the plan, throwing out polygonal bays to the garden front and at either end. The main room on the upper floor was the library, from which he could walk out beneath a free-standing portico and gaze at the monumental view, or shut himself away from the world with his books. Not that he held himself aloof on his Mount Olympus. "There is not a sprig of grass that shoots uninteresting to me," he writes. He took care of every detail of the running of Monticello, even when away from home on behalf of his government, as is shown by the copious instructions sent to his overseer.

THE SEMPLE HOUSE

FRANCIS STREET

COLONIAL WILLIAMSBURG FOUNDATION

The Semple House, which was also inspired by a plate owing its origins to Palladio's Redentore in Robert Morris's *Select Architecture*, has influenced the design of numerous houses in both North Carolina and Virginia. It is a perfectly balanced creation of correct and satisfactory proportions unusual for its date. The plan is symmetrical; a Great Hall in the center (nowadays divided) with the drawing room in one wing and the dining room in the other. The stairs are inconspicuous and of narrow proportions, in order to divert attention from the second storey and the basement. It is partly because of these features, typical of much of Jefferson's work, that the design of the house was for many years credited to him.

The facts regarding its ownership are somewhat shadowy, but a house of the same dimensions stood on its site at the time that the famous "Frenchman's Map" of Williamsburg was made in 1781. Thomas Tileston Waterman, in *The Mansions of Virginia*, published in 1946, feels that the design of the Semple House is closely akin to an early study for Monticello. This plan shows a large center block with one-room wings; the gable ends are marked as pedimented on the drawing. However, when Shadwell burned, on February 1, 1770, the records of Jefferson's architectural exercises prior to that date were destroyed, so that if he did indeed have anything to do with designing the house, no solid evidence of his involvement has survived.

Ten years previously, while attending the College of William and Mary, Jefferson was exposed to such architectural pattern books of the time as *Select*

The Semple House: Unique in Williamsburg, the Semple House is at the forefront of the Federal style which followed the Revolution. The Palladian influence is reflected in the classical symmetry of its façade.

Architecture and Gibbs's *Rules for Drawing*, and to the Leoni edition of Palladio's Four Books of Architecture. It was in these formative years that he began to think and to draw. Early sketches do survive, but none that antedate the burning of Shadwell and none that can be tied directly to the Semple House. Judge James Semple, who acquired the house at the end of the eighteenth century, gave it the name it bears to this day. Various owners have lived here since. This small Palladian house eventually came into the possession of Colonial Williamsburg and was one of its first restoration projects. Minor changes were erased, an addition was removed, and the house has been restored to perfection. It is still used as a private residence and is not open to the public.

RICHMOND

Jefferson was one of the chief proponents of the idea that the capital of the State of Virginia should be moved from the malarial climate of Williamsburg to a point nearer to the heart of the state. He put forward a bill to effect this in 1776, and although it was defeated, the state capital eventually was moved to Richmond in 1780. In his bill of 1776, Jefferson envisaged a series of government buildings "with walls of brick or stone, and Porticos where the same may be convenient or ornamental, and with pillars and pavements of stone." There was to be a house for the Governor, Courts of Justice, a "house for the use of the General Assembly to be called the Capitol" and a public market.

In 1780, Jefferson was appointed to head the committee of five Directors of the Public Buildings and sought to impose his taste and knowledge on the shape that Richmond was to take. His original scheme, however, was abandoned for reasons of economy. It was decided to put all the departments of the state government under one roof, and before leaving for Europe in 1784 Jefferson designed a capitol building for Richmond similar to that executed. When in France he commissioned C. L. A. Clérisseau, one of the leading architects in Paris, to make a model of his design, which is on display to this day in the Capitol at Richmond. Clérisseau had published a work entitled *Monuments de Nîmes* and was familiar with Jefferson's favorite building, the Maison Carrée. Jefferson writes: "I drew a plan for the interior, with the apartments necessary for legislative, executive, and judiciary purposes. . . . These were forwarded to the directors in 1786 and carried into execution." The model of the Capitol was shipped to Richmond in 1786 together with detailed plans for the interior. It resembles the Maison Carrée, which Jefferson had admired on paper in his edition of Palladio, but obviously it had to have windows, and the capitals are Ionic instead of Corinthian "on account of the difficulty of the Corinthian capitals."

Virginia State Capitol: The earliest recorded engraving. The portico was not erected until *ca.* 1790.

Virginia State Capitol: Working in Paris with C. L. A. Clérisseau, who had acted as guide and teacher to the brothers Adam in Rome, Jefferson had this model made. The design is basically that which appears in Jefferson's final studies as slightly modified by Clérisseau. The model arrived in Richmond in 1786.

Scale ¼ square = 1′   Virginia Capitol: End elevation - Study

Virginia State Capitol: Jefferson's drawing of his
scheme for this building, based on the Maison Carrée
at Nîmes, which he considered "the best morsel of
ancient architecture now remaining." The proportions are as recommended by Palladio.

Virgina State Capitol:
The Capitol in 1972.

Richmond, 1865: The State Secession Convention of
1861 met in the Capitol, and it was here that Robert
E. Lee accepted command of the Confederate forces.
Happily, the building escaped the devastation brought
to Richmond by the war.

Virginia State Capitol: The steps shown on Jefferson's drawing still had not been built when this view was taken in 1880.

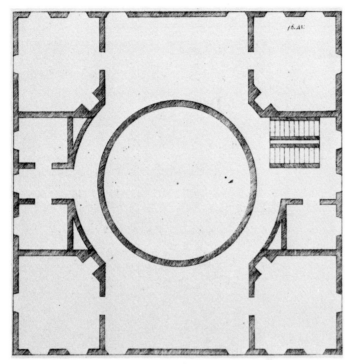

Plan for the second storey of the Governor's house.

Plan for the Governor's house, first floor: These drawings, done by Jefferson in about 1780, are studies for the Governor's house in Richmond. They show his interest in the Villa Rotunda as it appears in Palladio's Four Books of Architecture.

The Capitol at Richmond has been radically altered within, and wings have since been put on at either side to provide additional space; these inevitably detract from Jefferson's idea of a temple-form building. As such it was an innovation, although not the first building of this type to be designed by Jefferson. In 1779 he had proposed turning the Governor's Palace at Williamsburg into a classical temple. He probably considered it suitable that the new republic should look to Greece, mother of democracies, and to Rome for architectural inspiration. The new towns were being given classical names, such as Athens,

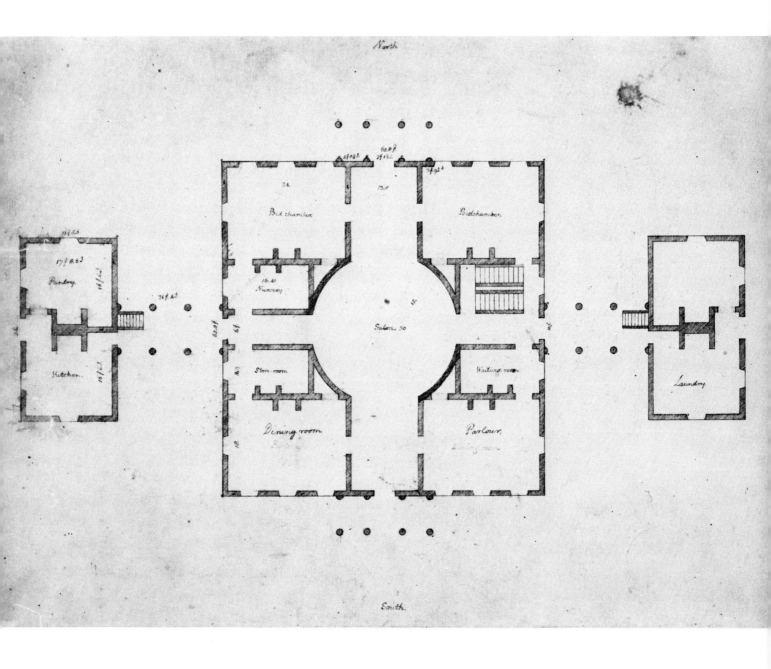

Palmyra, and Syracuse. In Jefferson's own household there were a slave named Caesar, and horses called Romulus and Remus, as well as the dog Ceres.

An elevated site was chosen. Old photographs of Richmond show the Capitol before the wings were added, and it seems to be suspended above the town, almost in the same way that the Parthenon dominates Athens. Originally there were no steps up to the front portico, adding to a feeling of remoteness that was anything but democratic; the building was entered through doors on either side. The interior does not appear to have retained any eighteenth-century features apart perhaps from some of the woodwork in the old Hall. There is an amusing story about the building of a small cantilevered staircase in the Capitol, sunk into the walls of a stairwell. It is said that workmen adamantly refused to remove the supports when it was completed, believing that the stair would collapse if they did.

Jefferson designed a residence for the state Governor which was a version of the Villa Rotunda at Vicenza. The design was rejected but it was not forgotten —he entered a similar drawing in the competition for the design of a house for the President in Washington in 1792.

There is a plan by Jefferson in the Coolidge Collection for the expansion of Richmond on the grid pattern which is neither an imaginative design, nor one suited to the hilly site. Later he was to advocate "building our cities on a more open plan": "Take, for instance, the chequerboard for a plan," which conformed with his love of symmetry and orderliness. "Let the black squares only be building squares, and the white ones left open, in turf and trees. Every square of houses will be surrounded by four open squares, and every house will front an open square. . . . The plan of the town . . . will be found handsome and pleasant." After his return from Europe, Jefferson had far more advanced theories as to the ideal townscape and was to be concerned with the development of Washington when he was Secretary of State and later on as President.

WASHINGTON

In its public buildings today, Washington reflects the influence of Grecian architecture rather than the Roman classicism that was to the taste of Thomas Jefferson. He was, however, to no small degree influential in the majestic development of the new Capitol, and had he not been burdened with affairs of state, his inventive genius would no doubt have found even more scope for expression. L'Enfant, a French artist and engineer, was commissioned to lay out the city in 1791, and indeed the bones of his design are still there. As a Frenchman, it was natural for him to favor straight vistas, fountains, and canals, and his noble concept was in the best tradition of his native country.

When Jefferson became President in 1801, he took steps to ensure that sufficient means were available to enable the public buildings then under way to be completed in a manner suited to the dignity of a capital city. His first practical achievement was the improvement of Pennsylvania Avenue, which leads from the White House to the Capitol. He divided it up with avenues of trees and footpaths in the manner of the great boulevards that he had seen and admired in France.

He created the post of Surveyor of the Public Buildings and gave it to Benjamin Latrobe, who was principally responsible for the Greek revival which soon swept across the nation. Latrobe writes to Jefferson in 1807: "My *principles* of good taste are rigid in Grecian architecture. I am a bigoted Greek in the condemnation of the Roman architecture of Baalbec, Palmyra, Spaletro, and of all the buildings erected subsequent to Hadrian's reign . . . wherever, therefore, the Grecian style can be copied without impropriety, I love to be a mere, I would say a *slavish* copyist." He worked on the Capitol during Jefferson's presidency, to the annoyance of William Thornton, whose plan had been selected after the competition in 1792.

Jefferson was himself an anonymous entrant in the original "President's

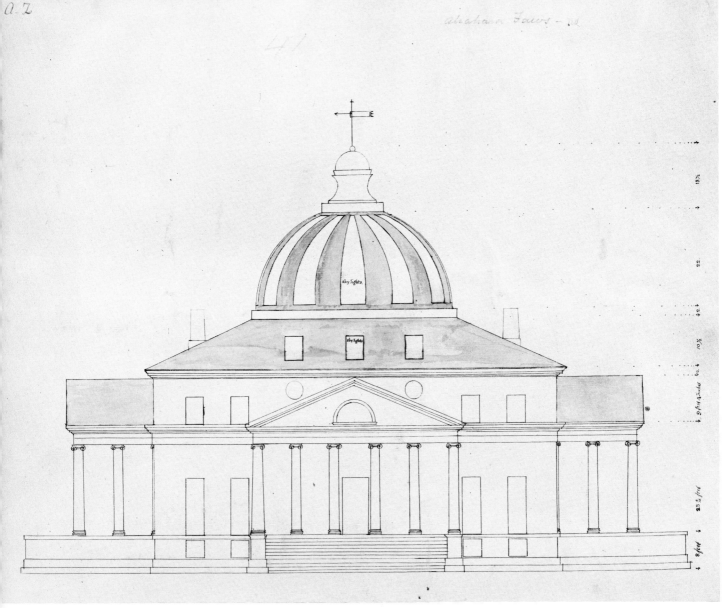

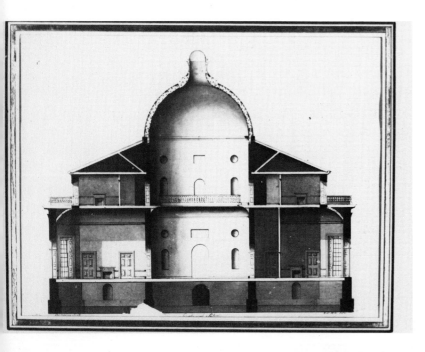

The "President's House": Mr. Jefferson's design for the President's Palace competition, in which he took second place. The drawing shows his continued interest in the scheme of the Villa Rotunda.

LEFT AND OPPOSITE: Another example of the influence of the Villa Rotunda. Robert Mills, who worked and studied for two years under Mr. Jefferson at Monticello, executed these drawings, which are believed to be studies for the rebuilding of Shadwell.

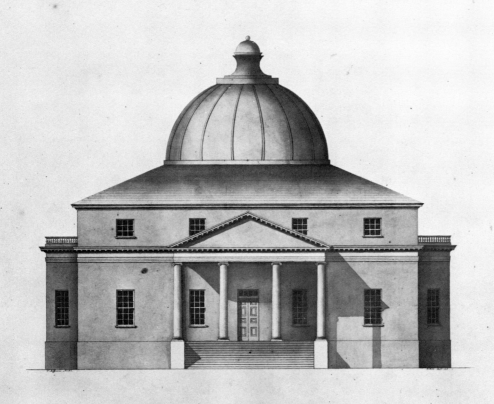

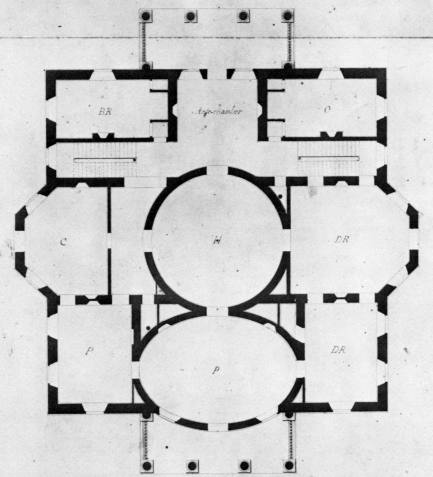

Palace" competition in 1792, signing his drawings "AZ." His design was a version of the Villa Rotunda, the dome surmounting a square block with seven bays on each of its four fronts. Each front was approached by a handsome flight of steps surmounted by a portico of six Ionic columns. How eminently fitting it would have been if he had won the competition and ten years later moved, as President, into a house of his own design.

The winning design was submitted by James Hoban, and the exterior of the President's House was finished more or less according to his plans, but while President, Jefferson designed the circular portico on the garden front, although it was not added until 1829. The interior was slowly completed under Jefferson's guidance, as many of the rooms still had to be plastered, and the grounds were laid out by Latrobe in close consultation with him. Jefferson designed colonnades, which now link the house with the executive offices, in 1804. Taking advantage of the groundfall, he planned a series of utilitarian offices, which were lacking in Hoban's chaste design, to be surmounted by a promenade—an echo of Monticello.

THE PETER CARR HOUSE

CHARLOTTESVILLE, VIRGINIA

DR. AND MRS. DAVID R. HAWKINS

The Peter Carr House, on the outskirts of Charlottesville, was built *ca.* 1794 by Peter Carr, Jefferson's favorite nephew; he was the son of Dabney Carr, a childhood friend who had married Jefferson's sister Martha. Major Thomas Carr, Dabney's grandfather, was the first to settle on the property, which overlooks the South Fork of the Rivanna River.

Peter Carr was born in 1770 and was only three when Dabney Carr died, whereupon Jefferson brought his widowed sister and all six of her children to live at Monticello. Peter was sent to the school of Mr. Walker Maury at Williamsburg. The school was moved into the old capitol building there in 1780, at the time the state government was transferred to Richmond. Peter Carr continued his education at the College of William and Mary and completed his law studies under George Wythe. For the next three years he read law in Goochland County, as Jefferson believed this would be more beneficial to him than serving an apprenticeship in a lawyer's office.

In 1793 Peter Carr began his law practice at Charlottesville, and it is thought that he began building his house the following year. Having been brought up at Monticello and educated directly across the street from the Semple House in Williamsburg, he was imbued with classical ideas in architecture at an early age. The house at Carrsbrook is a naïve, countrified version of the

The Peter Carr House (Carrsbrook): This building is a
Palladian exercise, the central block being flanked by wings
and pavilions. Jefferson often received guests here during
the remodeling of Monticello.

Semple House. Jefferson, particularly after his return from France, would certainly not have provided such an unsophisticated elevation, however delightful it may be in its own way. In its day, however, it was considered something of an innovation, and is included here because it demonstrates how far ahead Jefferson was of his contemporaries in the understanding of correct classical proportions.

It is apparent from an insurance policy of 1812, which includes an outline plan, that the house had a completely symmetrical frontage. A court was created in the rear by means of separate service buildings which stretched back, as if extensions of the wings. The front door leads directly into the Great Hall, now the drawing room. The four principal rooms face the entrance driveway, with the stairhall and service rooms behind, so as not to interfere with the view.

In 1804, Peter Carr was on the committee which was set up to amend the act establishing an academy at Charlottesville and to draft a bill for creating a state college, which afterwards became Central College. A private school was begun at Carrsbrook in 1811 but did not long survive. In 1814 five trustees met to consider the 1804 act, and Thomas Jefferson reminded them of the need for an institution of higher education. In this way the University of Virginia was born.

Carr died in 1815, and his heirs sold the house five years later. Several families have lived here since, and, as the city of Charlottesville has grown, the surrounding land has been sold off. Various unfortunate additions were removed by Dr. and Mrs. W. H. Paine in 1959, and the front has been returned to its eighteenth-century aspect once again.

MONTICELLO

When Jefferson returned from his five years abroad, his architectural taste had changed. He writes from Nîmes in March 1787 to the Comtesse de Tessé: "Here I am, Madam, gazing whole hours at the Maison Quarrée, like a lover at his mistress. The stocking weavers and silk spinners around it consider me a hypochondriac Englishman, about to write with a pistol the last chapter of his history. This is the second time I have been in love since I left Paris. The first was with a Diana at the Chateau de Laye-Epinaye in the Beaujolais, a delicious morsel of sculpture by Michael Angelo Slodtz. This, you will say, was in rule, to fall in love with a female beauty; but with a house! It is out of all precedent. No, Madam, it is not without a precedent in my own history. While in Paris, I was violently smitten with the Hôtel de Salm, and used to go to the Tuileries almost daily, to look at it. The *loueuse des chaises*, inattentive to my passion, never had the complaisance to place a chair there, so that, sitting on the parapet, and twisting my neck round to see the object of my admiration, I generally left it with a *torti-colli*." The dome, as well as the general massing, of the Hôtel de Salm, now the Palace of the Legion of Honor, provided the inspiration for the remodeling of Monticello.

"Were I to proceed to tell you how much I enjoy French architecture, I should want words." Jefferson had acquired a passion for the neoclassical architecture fashionable in France at that time. "The method of building houses 2, 3, or 4 stories high, first adopted in cities where ground is scarce, and thence without reason copied in the country, where ground abounds, has for these 20.

or 30. years been abandoned in all good houses newly built in the country, and very often even in the cities. In Paris particularly all the good and new houses are of a single storey. That is of the height of 16. or 18. f. generally and the whole of it given to the rooms of entertainment; but in the parts where there are bedrooms they have two tiers of them from 8. to 10. f. high each, with a small private staircase. By these means great staircases are avoided, which are expensive and occupy a space which would make a good room in every story. Nor is it a single storied house as expensive as those higher. . . ." When he re-

The Hôtel de Salm.

modeled Monticello, the house was lowered to give the appearance of having only one storey, and a dome was added. At the same time it was doubled in thickness so that, made to look smaller, it was in fact considerably enlarged. The new design was more sophisticated; his country house was transformed into a classical villa, abreast of European taste and filled with the ingenious contrivances which were the legacy of his inventive mind. While the reconstruction was in progress, Jefferson wrote to a prospective guest: "We shall have the eye of a brick kiln to poke you in or an octagon to air you in." In August of 1800,

Monticello, 1860.

MONTICELLO.

Monticello: Taken during renovation, this picture shows the pair of niches in the parlor. These details of the early Monticello are covered now by twin pier mirrors, which have been removed only once since their installation after arrival from France.

Mrs. Robert Liston, wife of the retiring British Ambassador and Minister Plenipotentiary, was touring the country with her husband. She writes of Monticello, which they had longed to see: "The top of the hill is flat, and the new building (the architecture is extremely fine) stands in the center of a pretty little lawn. Of the comfortable apartments of the house little can at present be said; none of the chambers are finished except a very small suite for his immediate use, consisting of a Bedchamber, Library, etc. I had never before seen Pictures and Mirrors placed upon bare brick walls; but Mr. Jefferson changes

Monticello: The plan of today's house, showing the depressed passages, service wings, and stables. The study, Jefferson's bedroom, the parlor, the dining room, and the tea room were in the original house.

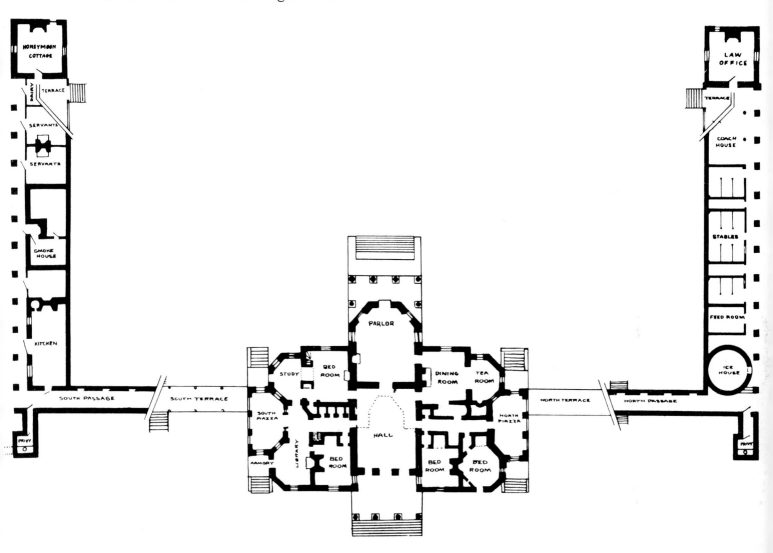

so often the ceilings, the floors, or partitions, that it cannot be otherwise."

The entrance hall was in Jefferson's time a sort of natural-history museum, such as may be found in many an English or Irish house. It was hung with the heads of animals brought back by Meriwether Lewis and William Clark from their mission to explore the West. Jefferson had ordered this expedition subsequent to the Louisiana Purchase from Napoleon in 1802. He was President at that date, and it was his vision and foresight that ensured this brilliant coup, much criticized at the time. Over the hall door there is a clock that tells the day

49

Monticello: "We have also run the collums for the South [East] Portico & I think they will when finished be elegant. . . ." Hugh Chisholm to Thomas Jefferson, September 4, 1808.

of the week as well as the hour; it is counterweighted by cannonballs from the Revolutionary War. The second Jeffersonian device to greet the visitor is an ingenious system for opening the double glass doors that lead into the parlor; by means of a chain under the floor, when one door is opened the other opens automatically at the same time. The hall contained a delightful mixture of things in his day: there was an Indian map of the Missouri drawn on buffalo hide hanging beside "The Repentance of St. Peter." There were some eighteen paintings and pieces of statuary, and a small collection of the fossil remains of great prehistoric animals, turned up when the site of the house was leveled. The room obviously had an atmosphere impossible to recreate, and which would in any case be anathema to the interior decorator of today.

The walls of the parlor beyond the hall were also crowded with paintings; in the year 1790 there were no less than forty-eight. The music stand, which could unfold for five musicians or fold back into a box, was Jefferson's invention. He also designed the parquet floor, the first of its kind in the United States, which was made of beech and cherry and was undoubtedly of French inspiration. In January 1827, after Jefferson died, most of the contents of the house were sold at auction, and although many things that belonged at Monticello have returned, much has been lost forever.

The library suite contains his architect's table, made in the Monticello cabinet-shop, and the polygraph with which he was able to make copies of his correspondence. Books that he owned have been given or purchased, and identical editions to those he was known to have on his shelves have been collected over the years to fill the bookcases. Jefferson's bed is set into an opening between his bedroom and his "cabinet" (one of the three rooms in the library suite), thus giving him access to it from both rooms, and improving the circulation of air in hot weather. His clothes were kept in the closet above the bed. He was an early riser, and for one who was up with the dawn it is perhaps curious that he designed for himself such a lofty and elaborate bedroom. It was his inner sanctum; here he could escape from his visitors and still be able to get at his books and also walk straight out into the garden beyond.

The dining room is also a double room, although in winter the wide opening into the tea room could be closed off for warmth. The color of the walls echoes that of the blue wedgwood plaques in the mantel. Concealed in the sides of this mantel are wine lifts that lead to the basement, and another Jefferson invention, found also at Bremo (q.v.), is the shelved door that gives onto the servery.

Thomas Jefferson died on July 4, 1826, fifty years to the day after the signing of the Declaration of Independence. Five years later Monticello, with the 552 acres remaining in the estate, was purchased for $7000 by a Charlottesville druggist, James T. Barclay, who intended to raise silkworms on the property.

Thomas Jefferson, by Gilbert Stuart.

OVERLEAF: Monticello, the entrance hall: ". . . went over to Monticello, I think the hall with its gravel coloured border is the most beautiful room I ever was in. . . ." Ellen Wayles Randolph to Thomas Jefferson, April 14, 1808.

The project failed, and in 1836 he sold the property to Uriah Levy for $2500.

Commodore Levy was a controversial figure, whose acrimonious relationship with the Navy Department was highlighted by a sensational court martial, from which he emerged fully vindicated but *persona non grata* with his superior officers. As a Jew, he had the greatest admiration for Jefferson. Levy wrote: "He did much to mold our Republic in a form in which a man's *religion* does not make him ineligible for political or governmental life." In 1833 he commissioned a statue of Jefferson to be presented to the nation; today it is the only piece of sculpture in the rotunda of the United States Capitol given by a private citizen. The year after Levy acquired Monticello he purchased 2502 additional acres for protection and started extensive repairs and restoration. Special attention was paid to the parquet floors, Jefferson's bedroom and cabinet, and Madison's room. The gardens were restored according to Jefferson's plans, and every effort was made to discover and repurchase original furnishings which had been dispersed. When he died, in 1862, Levy left Monticello to "the people of the United States." The will was unsatisfactory to his family in this and other respects, and after prolonged litigation was broken.

Joel Wheeler, who had been superintendent since 1839, stayed on after Levy's death and used the house as a residence, storage shed, cowbarn, and rubbish heap. Sarah N. Randolph closes her Preface to *The Domestic Life of Thomas Jefferson* (June 1871): "The view of Monticello represents the home of Thomas Jefferson as it existed during his lifetime, and not as it is now—a ruin." When Jefferson Levy, Uriah Levy's nephew, obtained possession of Monticello in 1881, Wheeler had to be forcibly evicted, and the second Levy restoration began, repairing the ravages of twenty years of neglect and maltreatment. Jefferson Levy was a New York lawyer and for two terms a member of Congress; he used Monticello as a summer home. President Theodore Roosevelt and other Washington notables visited him there, and he owned the house for more than forty years.

In 1923, on Jefferson's one hundred and eightieth birthday, the Thomas Jefferson Memorial Foundation purchased Monticello from Jefferson Levy for half a million dollars. Included in the sale were the hall clock, the folding ladder by which it was reached for winding, the pier mirrors in the parlor, and the pair of Sheraton card tables in the dining room. The aim of the foundation has been "to preserve rather than to restore, and to restore rather than to reconstruct." The measure of its momentous achievment can best be judged through the accompanying photographs. In spite of the thousands of visitors that come to see the house every year, the Thomas Jefferson Memorial Foundation has managed to preserve the unique personality of Monticello in memory of its creator.

Monticello: The west front.

Monticello, the entrance hall: Over a fireplace dating from the original building, the balcony connects the north and south sections of the second storey. The side chairs are believed to have been made in the plantation cabinet shop.

Monticello, the entrance portico: Turned by the weather vane on the roof, the wind dial in the ceiling is visible from eight rooms. The double-faced clock can be read from both inside and outside the house.

Monticello, the parlor: The French gilt mantel-clock, the Hepplewhite fire screens, the brass andirons, and the five paintings are original. The Louis XVI furniture is not, but is similar to that known to have been owned by Thomas Jefferson in Paris.

Monticello, the parlor: This view of the music corner of the parlor shows one of the French pier mirrors. The music rack and stand were probably made on the place; the pianoforte is believed to have been a gift from Jefferson to his daughter Martha.

Opposite: Monticello, the parlor: "The West room is finished in the manner which you told me...." Hugh Chisholm to Thomas Jefferson, September 4, 1808. The French doors open onto the west portico between busts of Napoleon and Alexander I of Russia.

Monticello, the parlor: The frieze in the parlor is from the Temple of Jupiter the Thunderer, from a book by Fréart de Chambray. The agricultural instruments represent the fertility of the earth; the sacrificial implements and "ox-sculls" represent the sacrifice of the bulls.

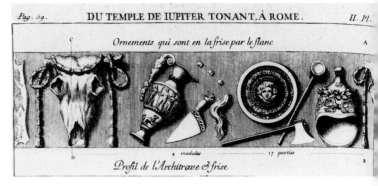

Monticello, the dining room mantel: "No nation is drunken where wine is cheap, and none sober, when the dearness of wine substitutes ardent spirits as the common beverage." At either end of the mantel is a dumb-waiter connected to the wine cellar below. The clock and figures are original Jefferson pieces.

Monticello, the dining room: This view looks toward the tea room; in the alcove to the right is the famous pivoting serving door. The two late Sheraton tables have never been out of the house since Jefferson owned them. A gourmet, Jefferson brought home from France a chef by the name of Petit to prepare the meals served in this elegant room.

Monticello, an upper bedroom: There were six rooms on the second storey, their windows placed at floor level so as to give the appearance from without of being a part of the windows below them.

Monticello, the south staircase: "I have done both of the stairways. . . ." Hugh Chisholm to Thomas Jefferson, September 4, 1808. The narrow treads and high risers achieve the suppressed stairs that Jefferson preferred.

Monticello, Jefferson's bedroom: Upon his return from Europe, Mr. Jefferson constructed the area for his bed and the closet above in this room, which was originally the size of the dining room. This was his *sanctum sanctorum;* few hands but his own opened the door to the entrance hall. The revolving chair, the table, and the long bench are original. The small table beside the bed is the only piece of furniture to survive the Shadwell fire.

Monticello, the book room: Mr. Jefferson's architect's table, made at Monticello, stands in this room. He no doubt stood at it to draw plans for the University and to design houses for his friends.

Monticello, the library: "I cannot live without books."

Monticello, the dome room: Sometimes called the "Sky Room." The exact intended use of the room beneath the dome is not known. At the time of Jefferson's death it was a storeroom.

Monticello, the west portico: Work was started on the dome, Mr. Jefferson's adaptation of the composition of the Hôtel de Salm, in 1800, and the columns of the portico were installed in 1802; but the work was not completed until 1808.

Monticello: "On the east side, . . . the eye is not checked by any object, since the mountain on which the house is seated commands all the neighboring heights as far as the Chesapeake." From a letter of the Duc de la Rochefoucauld.

"I remember you told me when we parted, you would come to see me at Monticello, and tho' I believe this to be impossible, I have been planning what I would shew you: a flower here, a tree there; yonder a grove, near it a fountain; on this side a hill, on that a river. indeed, madam, I know nothing so charming as our own country. the learned say it is a new creation; and I believe them; not for their reasons, but because it is made on an improved plan. Europe is a first idea, a crude production, before the maker knew his trade, or had made up his mind as to what he wanted."
—Thomas Jefferson

OVERLEAF: Monticello, Thomas Jefferson's grave: A new monument had to be erected after the original was defaced by vandals. It carries the original epitaph, as Mr. Jefferson himself wrote it.
Here was buried
Thomas Jefferson
Author of the
Declaration
of
American Independence
of the
Statute of Virginia
for
Religious Freedom
and father of the
University of Virginia

MONTPELIER

ORANGE COUNTY, VIRGINIA

MRS. MARION DUPONT SCOTT

The original house at Montpelier, which was of one storey, with two rooms on either side of the central hall, forms the core of the present mansion. It was built in the mid-eighteenth century by James Madison the elder, who was one of the richest men of his day in Orange County, although he did not choose to build an imposing house. In 1793, his son, shortly before his marriage to the legendary Dolley, sought architectural advice from Thomas Jefferson not only for himself at Montpelier but also for his brother at Woodberry Forest. Jefferson replies on May 19: "I have scribbled . . . some general notes on the plan of a house you enclosed. I have done more. I have endeavored to throw the same area, the same extent of walls, the same number of rooms, and the same sizes, into another form so as to offer a choice to the builder. Indeed, I varied my plan by showing what it would be with alcove bedrooms to which I am much attached." Madison thanked him for the letter, saying it was ". . . much approved and will be adopted by my brother." This must have been the design for Woodberry Forest, now the headmaster's house for the school that bears its name. Madison goes on to say: "I find I was misunderstood in my enquiry as to the proper width of the Portico. I did not mean the proportion it ought to bear to the side of the House to which it is attached: but the interval between the columns and the side of the House; or the distance which the Pediment ought to project. If there be any fixt rule on this subject, I will thank you to intimate it in your next." Jefferson's "fixt rule" is as follows: "A Portico may be from five to ten diameters of the column deep, or projected from the building. If of more than five diameters there must be a column in the middle of each flank,

73

Thomas Jefferson, by T. Kosciuszko: The
Polish hero of the American Revolution executed this portrait of his friend. In his
will, Kosciuszko left his American estate,
with Jefferson as executor, to be applied
toward freeing and educating Negro slaves.

Thomas Jefferson
A Philosopher a Patriote and a Friend
Dessiné par son Ami Tadée Kosciuszko.
Et Gravé par M. Sokolnicki

Montpelier: This early photograph shows the house before the wings were enlarged.

since it must never be more than five diameters from center to center of column. The Portico of the maison quaree is three intercolonnations deep. I never saw as much to a private house." It is clear that Jefferson designed the great portico at Montpelier, which is, in Fiske Kimball's words, "Jeffersonian in suggestion as well as in proportions." In 1804 the British minister visited Madison and noted, "There is a portico to it of the plainest and most massive order of architecture, but which Palladio gives us as a specimen of the Tuscan." In order to give the portico the proportions laid down by Jefferson, it was necessary to place the bases of the columns at ground level.

James Madison was elected to the Presidency in 1808, succeeding Thomas Jefferson, and in the following year he decided to enlarge Montpelier. Wings were added, the house was stuccoed and scored to resemble stone. There is a drawing in the Coolidge Collection of a Tuscan temple similar to the icehouse at Montpelier, suggesting that it may have been designed by Jefferson. Monticello has an icehouse, but they were by no means common at that date, and the one at Montpelier is among the first in its neighborhood.

Having served two terms as President, Madison retired to Montpelier in 1817. As a member of the Board of Visitors he attended the first legal meeting of the newly constituted Central College, together with Jefferson, Monroe, and General Cocke, the builder of Bremo. He was present on October 6, 1817, when the cornerstone was laid of the first pavilion of the college which became the University of Virginia. Madison spent the remainder of his life as a country gentleman, studying, farming, and gardening at Montpelier. He did everything on the grand scale, would entertain ninety people at lunch, and amassed such an enormous collection of books that he was crowded out of his library and had to do his reading elsewhere. Among his possessions was a portrait of Mr. Jefferson by Kosciuszko, which hung in the dining room; in the parlor at Monticello hung a Robert Edge Pine portrait of Madison (since lost), which had been there since 1792.

Madison died on June 28, 1836. After his death Dolley Madison moved to Washington and was later obliged to sell the plantation. She rests today in the family graveyard at Montpelier, near her husband. The property was eventually purchased by the father of the present owner—it was Mr. duPont who raised the Madison wings and further extended the house. Montpelier has long been a respected name in Thoroughbred-breeding and steeplechasing circles; every autumn a Hunt Race meeting is held on the estate.

BELLE GROVE

Middletown, Virginia

The National Trust for Historic Preservation

In 1782 or 1783, Major Isaac Hite received from his father some five hundred acres in Frederick County, a portion of a large land grant made to his grandfather with a view to encouraging settlement in the Shenandoah Valley. Shortly after taking possession of his inheritance, Hite married Eleanor Madison of Montpelier, the sister of James Madison. The future President and his young wife, Dolley, were paying a bride-visit to "my sister Hite" when he wrote to his father (October 5, 1794) that he and Major Hite had discussed the building of a more elegant house on the property. Two days later he writes to his friend Thomas Jefferson: "On my return to Orange I dropped you a few lines on the subject of the deer. On my way to this part of the country I passed Col. John Thorntion of Culpeper, who has a Park, and will spare you with pleasure two or three, if you cannot be otherwise supplied. He thinks he could by advertising a premium of 10 or 12 dollars a head procure from his neighbors as many fawns to be delivered to Monticello as you would want. If you choose to make use of his assistance, a line to the care of Mr. Fontaine Maury at Fredg would soon get to hand.

"This will be handed to you by Mr. Bond who is to build a large house for Mr. Hite my brother in law. On my suggestion he is to visit Monticello not only to profit of examples before his eyes, but to ask the favor of your advice on the plan of the House. Mr. Hite particularly wishes it in what relates to the [Bow] ?-room & the Portico, as Mr. B. will explain to you. In general, any hints which may occur to you for improving the place will be thankfully ac-

Belle Grove, the south front.

Belle Grove, the entrance doorway.

"Belle Grove house—General Sheridan's H'd Qts. at Cedar Creek . . .
Gordon's troops sweeping the 19th Corps before it by the house at dawn."
From the Sketchbook and Diary of James E. Taylor, who was attached to
the staff of General Philip H. Sheridan during the 1864 campaign.

cepted. I beg pardon for being the occasion of this trouble to you, but your good-
ness has always so readily answered such draughts on it, that I have been
tempted to make this additional one.

"I write at present from the desk of Mr. G. Washington of Berkeley, where,
with a succession of town visits, I have remained since the 15th ult; The speed
with which I had the happiness to accomplish the alliance which I intimated
to you I had been some time soliciting. We propose to set out in 8 or 10 days for
Philada where I shall always receive your commands with pleasure, and shall
continue to drop you a line as occasions turn up. In the mean time I remain yr,
Mo: affecly. J. Madison, Jr."

Belle Grove was built of local limestone; the dressed stone of the south façade
added about one-third to the cost of the masonry. In the collection of papers
given to the National Trust by Francis G. Olmstead, appears "W. Williamsons
calculation" for the masonry work. In addition to the cutting, setting, and point-
ing of walls, chimneys, etc., sixteen days' work was required for the stone pillars supporting the portico floors and their wooden Doric columns. Belle Grove
appears to reveal more of an English influence than was normal in its locality,
where the German settlers had introduced their own somewhat heavier style.

According to J. K. Paulding: "The houses are of stone and built for duration, not for show. If a German builds a house its walls are twice as thick as others, if he puts down a gatepost, it is sure to be nearly as thick as it is long. Everything about him, animate and inanimate, partakes of this character of solidarity. His wife is even a jolly, portly dame, his children chubby rogues, with legs shaped like old-fashioned mahogany bannisters, his barns as big as fortresses, his horses like mammoths, his cattle enormous."

The building work must have been well under way by the first of May, 1795, as an order for yellow pine, "interior finish lumber," was to be delivered to the site by that date. Exactly a year later, during a two-week visit to Philadelphia, Major Hite spent over £2000 for six hundred items needed for the completion of Belle Grove; finishing hardware, tools, window glass, paint, furnishings, and so forth. Papers have recently come to light that provide a fascinating record of the building of this "frontier" house toward the end of the eighteenth century. The survival of these documents is little short of miraculous, to judge from the following account from David Strothers' Civil War Journal (May 11, 1864):

"Tents struck and the army moved southward toward Strasburg. Graves and dead animals in all stages of decomposition marked the way. We took headquarters at the house of Isaac Hite on Cedar Creek between Middletown and Strasburg, the same house where Fremont had his headquarters when he was relieved of his command in 1862. The old house of cut limestone is of baronial size and was built many years ago in the style of the old Virginia mansions of the colonies. Hite was one of those who squatted on Lord Fairfax's manor, and in the garret were found barrels of old papers illuminating the history of the family, neighborhood, and times of Lord Fairfax. There were some autograph letters, receipts, and business letters of Thomas Jefferson and George Washington, besides many other names famous in their day. As the house was only occupied by a poor family of tenants, our officers helped themselves to these literary mementos. The ample oak floors of the dwelling afforded us bedroom and office room, while a semicircle of tents was pitched in the front lawn under an immense lilac hedge in full bloom. A most beautiful and fragrant shade. Here we remained for several days."

The Doric portico is a typical Jefferson detail, as is the fanlight over the front door. Like several other of his designs, Belle Grove has a T-shaped hall and minor stairs. There is essentially one living storey with service rooms below; the kitchen appears always to have been in the basement. Outbuildings included the dairy and the smokehouse. The wing is later than the body of the house, and is of uncertain date, but it appears in a contemporary sketch of General Sheridan's headquarters at Cedar Creek in the fall of 1864. In an inventory of 1851, seven rooms are listed in the main house: dining room, parlor, entry, chamber, nursery, bedroom, yellow room, and a small storeroom. Although the conception of Belle Grove is Jeffersonian, the interior detail is more transitional, from Georgian to Federal. In the southwest room, the fireplace has the heavy back-band around the masonry opening often found in Jefferson's houses; the rest of the room is of an earlier fashion. The parlor is somewhat more elegantly conceived, in the style of the brothers Adam.

Isaac Hite's second wife lived on until 1851. Belle Grove was sold in 1860 and during the War between the States saw the tides of battle come and go. Had it not served as temporary quarters or headquarters for several generals of the Union forces, including Sheridan during the scorched-earth campaign of 1864, it might well have been burned, as were so many of its neighbors. There have been many owners of the property since the time of the Hites. In 1964, Belle Grove was accepted by the National Trust as a gift from the estate of the late Francis Welles Hunnewell, who had owned it since 1929. It is now maintained by the trust as a house museum, and is open to the public.

Edgehill: After Jefferson's death, the bulk of his papers and drawings was brought here, and in 1898 a large collection of them was presented to the Massachusetts Historical Society by his great-grandson, Thomas Jefferson Coolidge. Jefferson's daughter Martha lived here in a storey-and-a-half frame house, later moved back by her son, who built the lower floor of this house on the plantation adjoining Shadwell.

FARMINGTON

CHARLOTTESVILLE, VIRGINIA

FARMINGTON COUNTRY CLUB

Farmington is beautifully situated astride a high and broad knoll, with panoramic views of the surrounding countryside and the Blue Ridge Mountains. It has been in use as a country club for the last forty-five years, so that the building and grounds have been properly cared for. No doubt in Jefferson's day the house stood in the midst of parkland, with grazing cattle and horses, the "controlled nature" that he most admired. Jefferson's views on ideal surroundings were as definite as those he held on architecture. He did not, for instance, care for the gardens at Blenheim in England, which are in a sense an extension of the house into the outdoors; after going to visit them in 1786 he wrote: "Art appears too much."

The Farmington estate was purchased by George Divers, a friend of Jefferson's, in 1785. The existing house was modest in size, of two storeys, with a side hall plan, and it lacked an imposing frontispiece. In 1802 Divers decided to enlarge it and wrote to Jefferson for advice. In spite of the fact that he was then President, Jefferson found time to draw an ingenious plan; his original drawing for it is preserved in the Coolidge Collection. His idea was to double the house in size by putting on a handsome addition in the form of an elongated octagon, fronted by a Doric portico.

It has already been shown, at Monticello and elsewhere, that by this date Jefferson had a preference for the one-storey house. At Ampthill he suggested the frontispiece of one storey, added to the older two-storey house, linking them in such a way as to form an H-shaped plan. At Farmington, Jefferson was able

Farmington.

Farmington: The drawing room as it exists today with new and old partitions removed so that it occupies all of Mr. Jefferson's addition.

to minimize the effect of the second storey in the addition by the use of *oeil de boeuf* windows. Kimball has proved beyond reasonable doubt that these were the identical windows that Jefferson had ordered for himself from London in 1792 but never used. As at Monticello, the Doric portico carries an elaborate cornice which is continued around the octagon to either side.

On July 14, 1803, George Divers writes to Jefferson: "Soon after the receipt of your favor of the 18th May inclosing a drawing of an architrave frieze and cornice for my two fireplaces, I wrote you that the frieze boards must be 5 f. 7 inches by 7½ inches in place of 5 f. 4 I. by 6 I. As soon as they are ready and the composition ornaments are done, be so good as to direct them to be shipped. . . . My workmen have but very little to do and I fear I will be waiting for the ornaments. If the man who did some plastering for you or any other good plasterer can be engaged to come out here from the city of Washington I shall be glad to employ one to plaster my two Rooms passage and Columns, perhaps you may also have a Room or two ready. I shall be ready by the middle or the last of August at farthest. I must ask the favor of you to engage a good hand to come out; and advise me by post, when he will be here or whether such a man can be engaged or not. . . ."

George Divers fell ill, and Jefferson went to Farmington to inspect the building progress on his behalf during the course of a visit to Charlottesville. He considered the workmen unsatisfactory and had them dismissed. Divers' illness proved fatal, and the addition was not finally completed for fifty years, by which time the property was in the possession of General Bernard Peyton. According to Jefferson's plan, the octagon was to have had only two large rooms; General Peyton, however, divided it into four rooms with a central hall. Today it is one huge chamber, two storeys in height, and of magnificent proportions which make a dramatic impact on the visitor. Jefferson could not but approve the deviation from his plan were he to see this great room today.

EDGEMONT

North Garden, Virginia

Mr. and Mrs. Parker Snead

Houses with four porticos are few and far between in any country, and Edgemont in its simple understatement of the Palladian villa demonstrates Jefferson's theory of design. In 1784 he writes in his *Notes on Virginia*, discussing the majority of private houses in the state: "It is impossible to devise things more ugly, more uncomfortable, and happily more perishable. . . . Buildings are often erected by individuals of considerable expense. To give these symmetry and taste would not increase their cost. It would only change the arrangement of the materials, the form and the combination of the members. This would often cost less than the burden of barbarous ornaments with which these buildings are sometimes charged. But the first principles of the art are unknown, and there exists scarcely a model among us sufficiently chaste to give an idea of them." Its faultless proportions lend Edgemont the elegance of a palace and the simplicity of a cottage. It is the perfect example of how purity of line can be used to best advantage.

The design of Edgemont is not in fact quite as straightforward as it first appears. The attendant flanking pavilions, erected on existing foundations at a later date, are not immediately apparent; as they are linked to the house by underground passages it takes a moment before the eye can take in that they are a part of the architectural scheme. A perfect balance has been achieved between house and dependencies that lends it an unforgettable magic and serenity.

Jefferson designed Edgemont in 1797 for Colonel James Powell Cocke, and the original plans are in the Coolidge Collection, numbers 171 to 174, identified by Milton Grigg in 1935. The site is fairly steep, and at the front only one

Edgemont: The west front.

Edgemont: The drawing room.

Edgemont: The entrance hall. An original mantel was moved here from the drawing room, and the screen was introduced in accordance with evidence of an earlier screen found on the ceiling and floor.

Edgemont: The west front before restoration.

Edgemont: Mr. Jefferson's drawing, showing the fourth portico, which was not in fact completed until the restoration of the 1940s.

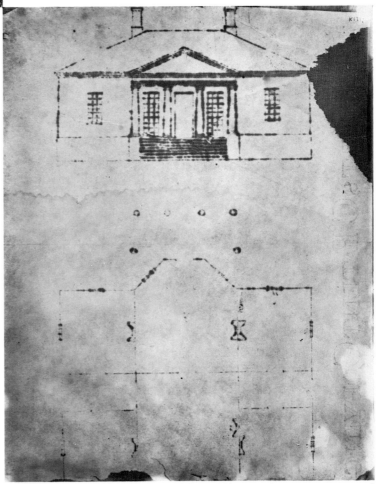

Edgemont: The garden front.

storey is shown, whereas at the back there are two. The drawing room is octagonal and projects into the portico, which looks out over the garden. The choice of an elevated site was not, in this case, accidental. James Cocke had exchanged his home, Malvern Hill in Henrico County, for this land in Albemarle County because he suffered from malaria and the benefits of mountain air had been recommended for his complaint. It is unlikely that Jefferson would have suggested that Cocke build a frame house, for in the *Notes on Virginia* he makes his views on the subject clear: "The private buildings are very rarely constructed of stone or brick, much the greater portion being of scantling and boards, plastered with lime." He attributes the root of the evil to the "unhappy prejudice" that houses of brick or stone are less wholesome than those of wood. "A dew is often observed on the walls of the former in rainy weather, and the most obvious solution is, that the rain has penetrated through these walls." He argues that "the inhabitants of Europe, who dwell chiefly in houses of stone or brick, are surely as healthy as those of Virginia. . . . A country whose buildings are of wood, can never increase in it's improvements to any considerable degree." The choice of building materials at Edgemont, however, is a particularly happy one, the snow-white house framed against the blue Virginia sky, its feet in the dark green garden below, although it is the only frame house known to have been designed by Jefferson.

After Colonel Cocke's death the house passed to his eldest son's widow, and then to her heir, Judith A. Randolph. It was then lost from view, and neither Fiske Kimball nor I. T. Frary, whose works on Jefferson's architecture appeared in 1916 and 1931 respectively, mention its existence. There was a succession of owners from 1862 to 1937, the Yates family having the longest tenure. There was an illicit still in the house during Prohibition, and some gold is said to have been buried nearby at the time of the Civil War. The strangest of all stories concerns the Misses Yates, two spinster sisters who had lived together all their lives. When one of them died the other was heartbroken, and her grief led her to curious extremes of mourning. Not only did she dress in black, as would have been expected; she had the entire house painted black, both inside and out! During the recent restoration, evidence of the truth of this tale was found.

Milton Grigg, the architect and restorer, together with Frances Johnston the photographer, came upon Edgemont at the eleventh hour. Agnes Rothery, in *Houses Virginians Have Loved* (whence the information above comes) records that "the building itself was in a state of collapse: a grass fire had erased the gardens . . . weeds covered the yard, erosion had shattered the terraces. It was not until later, with the exploratory digging of trenches in search of original ground lines, that the conformation of the terraces, the ramps and the shallow rise of the bowling green were revealed."

The task of restoration was begun by Mr. Grigg for Dr. Graham Clarke, who bought the property in order to rescue it in 1936, but when the war came the work was discontinued. In 1946 it came into the hands of Mr. and Mrs. William Snead, whose son now owns the property. The Sneads have restored Edgemont to perfection, and in so doing have saved for posterity a house which is perhaps the most exquisite example of Jefferson's entire *oeuvre*.

POPLAR FOREST

FOREST, VIRGINIA

MR. AND MRS. JAMES WATTS, JR.

Poplar Forest stands on land that came to Jefferson as part of his wife's inheritance, and he built himself a refuge here so that he could escape from all the comings and goings at Monticello. In a letter from Washington, dated April 27, 1806, Jefferson writes that he is "preparing an occasional retreat in Bedford, where I expect to settle some of my grandchildren." Poplar Forest, as he called the house, was ninety miles from his "little mountain," and it was enjoyed regularly by Jefferson from the time of his first recorded visit there in September 8, 1773, until his last in the spring of 1823.

The plan for the present building took shape during his second term as President. He had designed an octagonal house for his daughter Maria at Pantops, an estate near Monticello which he had given her in 1797 as her dowry. Construction there was stopped on her untimely death in 1804. Jefferson used the same plan, somewhat modified, when work began at his new house on the Bedford County plantation in 1806. On June 16 of that year he writes to his daughter, Martha Jefferson Randolph, "I will have to proceed to Bedford almost without stopping in Albemarle. I shall probably be there a week or ten days, laying the foundation of the house. . . ." In 1807: "Get from Mr. Perry and Mr. Dinsmore an estimate of all the nails we shall want for the house in Bedford." In 1810 there were spring, summer, and winter trips in order to expedite the completion of the house. In August of the next year he writes, from Poplar Forest, "I have fixed myself comfortably, keep some books here, bring others occasionally, am in the solitude of a hermit and quite at leisure to attend to my

Poplar Forest: The garden elevation, which was drawn
about 1820 by Cornelia Jefferson Randolph.

absent friends." During the summer of 1814 most of the interior was completed, and a wing of offices 110 feet long was built. In 1819 Jefferson spent two months of the summer here, supervising the plastering of the dining-room ceiling and the laying of a marble hearth, and he also paid a visit here in April 1820. Although not then in the best of health, he was active enough, much of his time being devoted to the University, where by September of 1820 seven pavilions and about thirty dormitories were nearing completion.

In 1727 William Kent published a book of *Designs of Inigo Jones* which contains a plan* for an octagonal house that is probably the source for Poplar Forest, although it is rather more elaborate. The house is an octagon, each side fifty feet in length. In the center there is a square two-storey dining room, surrounded by four lozenge-shaped spaces. On the north, leading from the en-

* Vol. II, Plate 17.

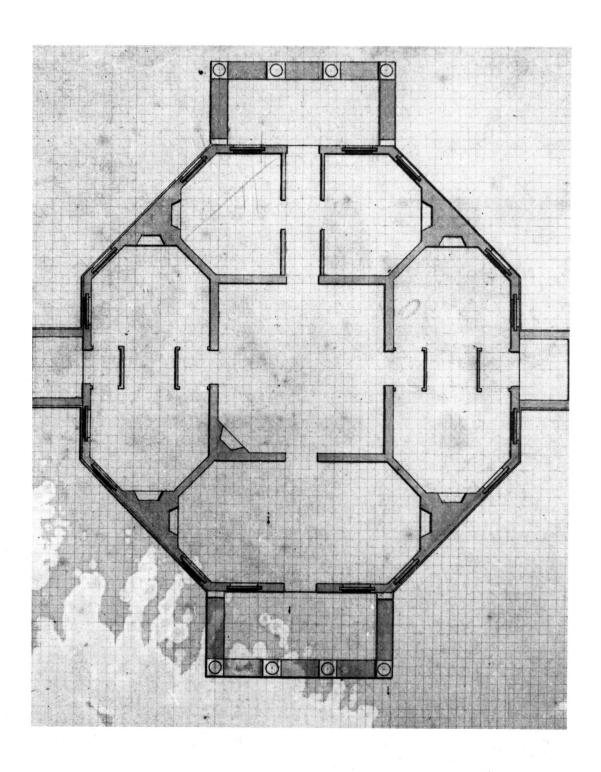

Poplar Forest: The main floor plan, drawn by Cornelia
Randolph, was probably based on an Inigo Jones scheme
for an octagonal house.

Poplar Forest: One of the twin octagonal necessary houses.

Poplar Forest: The southwest elevation of the house.

Poplar Forest: The living room cornice, based on one in Pavilion II at the University, was installed by the present owners.

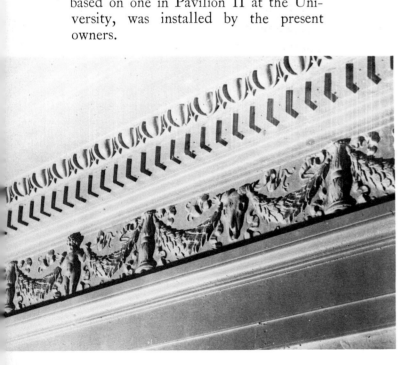

Poplar Forest: The living room.

Poplar Forest: The north portico, which survived the fire and is the main entrance to the house.

trance portico, there is a narrow hall which divides one of these areas. The plans show that the east and west lozenges were divided in the center by sleeping alcoves, arranged so as to allow access from either side, as in Jefferson's own bedroom at Monticello. The remaining space on the south forms an octagonal living room, which gives onto the south portico overlooking the garden. Stairs were located in small projections on the east and west faces of the house, one leading to Jefferson's private apartment and the other to a pantry. Service rooms were on the lower floor, and under the south portico there is a basement arcade where the land falls away. The house shows one storey on the entrance front and two on the garden side, like Edgemont or the extant building at Barboursville. The earth that was scooped out to make a sheltered lawn at the lower level provided material for two symmetrical mounds to either side, which served to screen the two octagonal necessary houses.

Life at Poplar Forest was much less formal than at Monticello; otherwise the use of the central space as a dining room would not have been permissible. Jefferson also allowed himself liberties in the interior detail. In a letter to the ornamentist W. J. Coffee in New York (July 10, 1822) regarding ornaments for the friezes, he writes: "In my middle room at Poplar Forest, I mean to mix the faces and ox-sculls, a fancy I can indulge in my own case, although in a public work I feel bound to follow authority strictly." The Peaks of Otter were visible from the house, and Jefferson determined to measure them "to gratify a common curiosity as to the height of those mountains, which we deem our highest."

Fire gutted the main house in 1845, and at the time of the reconstruction the elevations were altered. The central skylight and balustrade were omitted, the new cornice lacked character, dormer windows were inserted into the roof, and the pediment on the south portico was not restored. Fulfilling a childhood dream, the present owner purchased Poplar Forest in 1947 and began the process of restoring the house more nearly to its original form. Windows which had been bricked up were opened, and a living room cornice based on one at the University was made up and installed. Some day the south pediment will be put back, and this unusual house will once more stand in all its Jeffersonian glory.

FARMINGTON

LOUISVILLE, KENTUCKY

THE HISTORIC HOMES FOUNDATION

Fiske Kimball, writing in 1916, put forward the theory that three of Jefferson's drawings in the Coolidge Collection were studies for Poplar Forest (*q.v.*), a house which was built in the shape of an octagon. They show a plan evolving, the most elaborate having a symmetrical balance of octagons and porches. Mr. Milton Grigg, the architect who has devoted half a lifetime to the restoration of Jeffersonian buildings, has recognized the fact that these were drawings for Farmington, Kentucky. Kimball agreed with this, and wrote in 1950: ". , . the essential scheme of this plan of Jefferson's, unique in his work, is its having the two octagonal rooms back to back and separated by a hall, and each flanked by square bedrooms within a generally square mass of fifty by sixty feet . . . whoever modified the plans was evidently a competent builder, for the changes are ingenious." The main deviation from Jefferson's plan was in the elongation of the octagonal rooms, resulting in a passage which is rather narrow and dark in spite of the interior fanlight.

Stone steps lead up to the main floor, where all the principal rooms are situated, with ceilings that are fourteen feet high. Extremely narrow stairs lead down to the basement, which is well lit, being for the most part above ground—and the only ornament is in the window trim and handsome mantels; their absolute plainness, immense height, and excellent proportions give them a spacious and elegant effect.

Farmington was built for Judge John Speed on a tract of land that had been granted to his father, Captain James Speed, in 1785. John Speed knew Jefferson well. His second wife was Lucy Fry, great-granddaughter of Joshua Fry,

Farmington, Kentucky: The entrance front.

who was Peter Jefferson's partner in producing the map of Virginia (see end-paper). Lucy's grandfather was Dr. Thomas Walker, the guardian of Thomas Jefferson. Her aunt was married to George Divers of the other Farmington, near Charlottesville, for which Jefferson had designed an addition in 1802. Farmington, Kentucky, was called after its namesake in Virginia, and it may have been through George Divers that the plans were obtained.

Building work began on the house shortly after the marriage of John and Lucy Speed in 1808; the plantation was able to supply most of the building materials—limestone, timber, and clay for the bricks. It took two years to complete. Among the most famous visitors to the house was Abraham Lincoln, who came here in 1841 to recover from a rift in the course of his turbulent courtship of Mary Todd, and stayed for some weeks. One of the seventy-odd plantation slaves was attached to him as a personal servant, and he was also provided with his own horse. He was an old friend of Joshua Fry Speed, the son of John and Lucy. Together they "tramped the fields, took long rides into the country, and chatted with the gentle, philosophic Mrs. Speed." He enjoyed nothing more than the "dishes of peaches and cream" and remembered them for the rest of his life. What better cure for a broken heart?

The house remained in the possession of the Speed family until 1865, after which there was a succession of owners. In 1957 it was acquired by the Historic Homes Foundation of Louisville, Kentucky, and the house and garden have now been restored and made open to the public. Farmington provides an ideal setting for the period furniture and pictures that have been assembled for display here.

BARBOURSVILLE

BARBOURSVILLE, VIRGINIA

MR. AND MRS. C. FRANCIS SMITHERS

Barboursville stands as a majestic ruin, surrounded by lawns and flowering trees. It caught fire on Christmas Day, 1884, but fortunately the remains of the brick walls and the two porticos have been preserved and today provide the focal point of interest in the gardens.

Thomas Jefferson designed the house for Governor James Barbour. His original drawing, in the Coolidge Collection, has been dated 1817, and there are many features in the plan reminiscent of Jefferson's own home at Monticello. There was to have been a dome, which was never built, and the windows were grouped together so as to make the two storeys appear to be one. The octagonal drawing room, which was two storeys high, projected into the garden portico, the entrance hall was the same height as the drawing room; the staircases were contained in the two transverse passages.

Barboursville had the usual fireplaces on the first floor, and the upper rooms were heated by Franklin stoves, as at the University of Virginia, which was also building in 1817. Governor Barbour sent his master workmen to Monticello to study Jefferson's building methods at first hand, and it is probable that they visited the site of the University at the same time. In March 1817 he writes to Jefferson: "The bearers of this, James Bradley and Edward Ancel are the undertakers of my building—the former a carpenter—the latter a bricklayer. I have resolved on the plan you were good enough to present me and for which I return you my sincere thanks. You were kind enough to accompany the plan with a

Barbboursville: An early painting shows the house as it was before the fire.

Barboursville: The service buildings before restoration.

Barboursville: The service buildings, restored and joined to make today's manor house.

OVERLEAF: Barboursville: Thomas Jefferson's drawing of the plan and entrance elevation, showing the proposed dome, which was never built.

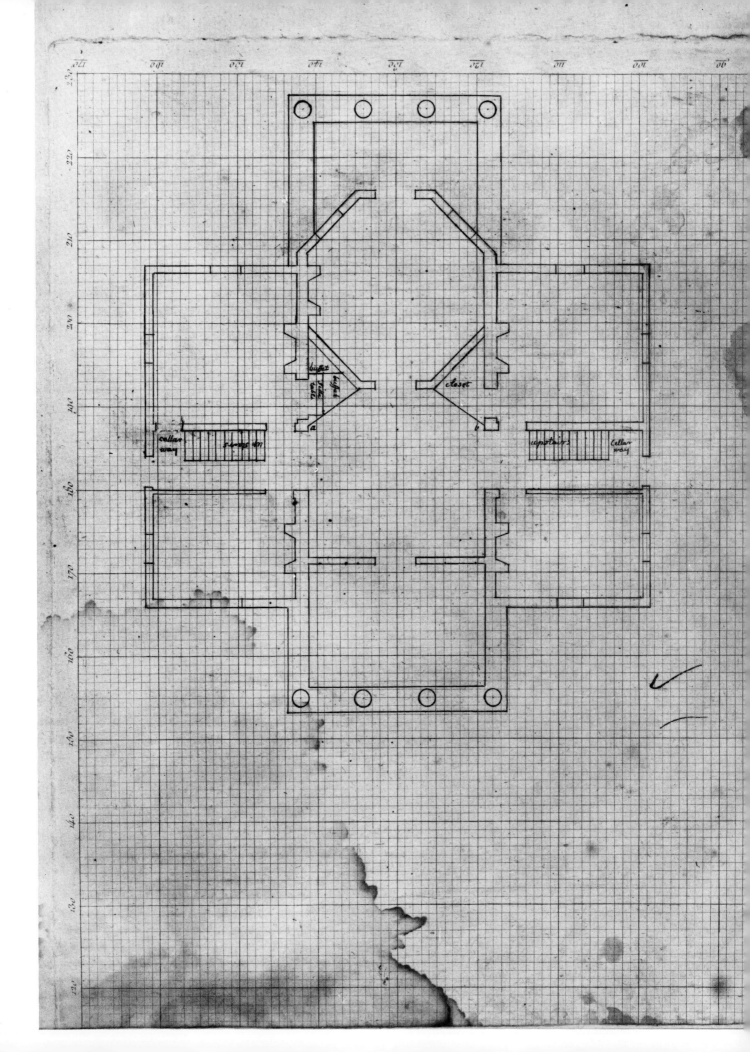

cellar
way

upstairs

cellar
way

buffet

closet

a

b

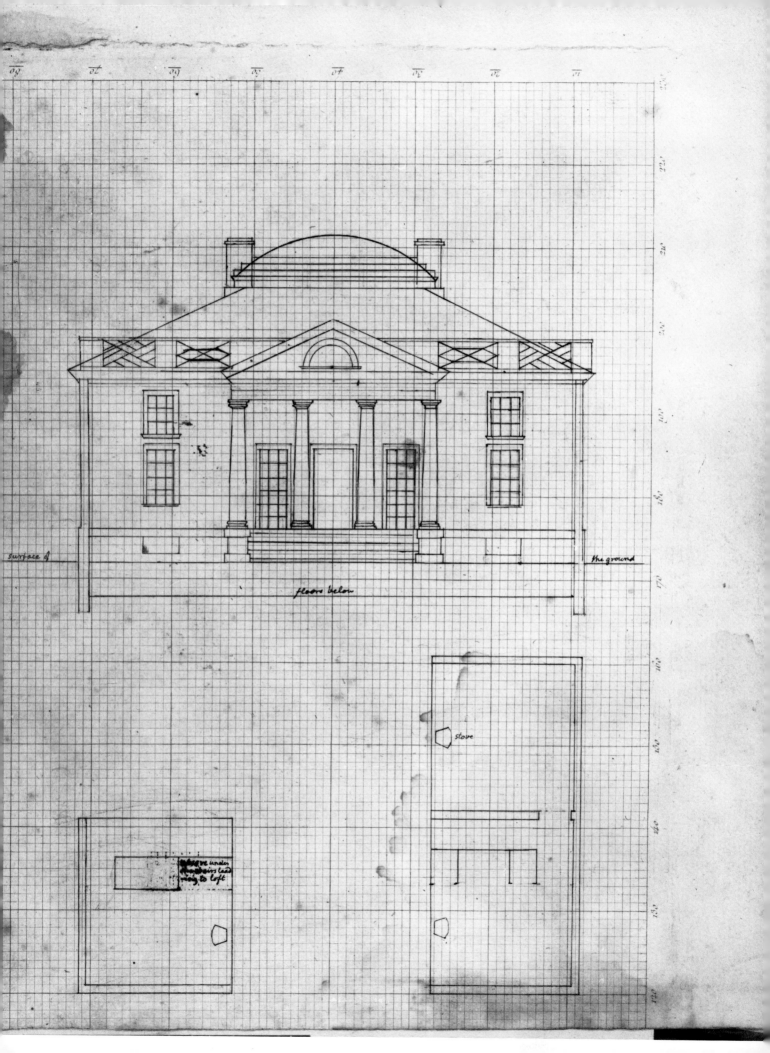

surface of   the ground

floors below

stove

above under
the stairs lead
ing to loft

suggestion that it would be well for my workmen to see your building and receive such verbal explanations as might facilitate their labors. To that end I have directed them to repair to Monticello. . . ."

The service buildings, now the main residence, are at the west end of the house. These had been built in 1790, and Jefferson may have planned another range on the east side, to balance the composition and satisfy his love of symmetry. They show one storey on the entrance court but in fact contain two full floors. Fortunately these buildings survived the fire, and were subsequently joined together and made into living quarters for the family. Barboursville remained in the hands of the original family until it was sold in 1947. It is still a working plantation, particularly known for Mr. Smithers' remarkable flock of Hampshire Down sheep.

Barboursville: The ruins.

THE UNIVERSITY OF VIRGINIA

CHARLOTTESVILLE, VIRGINIA

*Thomas Jefferson still survives.**

The design of the University of Virginia will live forever. It was the first instance in America of Visionary Architecture, that curious offshoot of the classical revival in France that flourished, though somewhat more on paper than in terms of bricks and mortar, at the close of the eighteenth century. Not only was Jefferson a visionary; he had the determination to see his dream become a reality and the strength of purpose to carry through his grandiose scheme. He was seventy-three when the cornerstone on the first pavilion was laid, and impatient with the constant delays attendant on any official undertaking. In order to hasten the work, for instance, he ordered carved capitals from Italy before the expenditure had in fact been sanctioned. He had the satisfaction of living long enough to see the doors of the University opened to students for the first time on March 7, 1825.

The agent or overseer at Monticello, Captain Bacon, recalled that Jefferson, a professional lawyer if an amateur architect, wrote the deed for the purchase of the land himself and lost no time in laying out the ground. Bacon writes:

* Last words of his friend President John Adams, who, in fact, outlived Jefferson by only twelve hours.

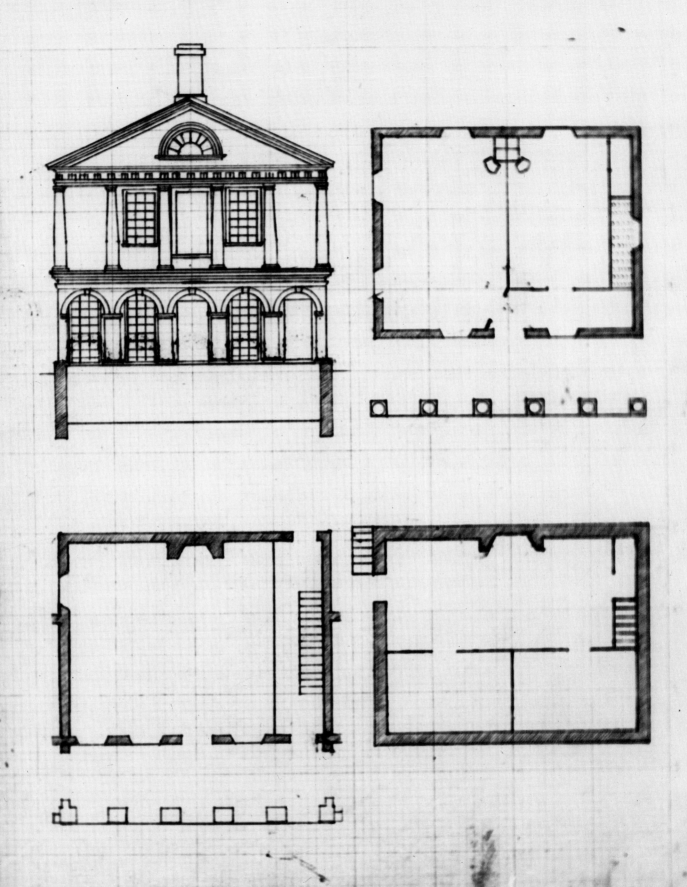

Pavilion Nᵒ VII. w. Doric Palladio.

THE UNIVERSITY OF VIRGINIA

CHARLOTTESVILLE, VIRGINIA

*Thomas Jefferson still survives.**

The design of the University of Virginia will live forever. It was the first instance in America of Visionary Architecture, that curious offshoot of the classical revival in France that flourished, though somewhat more on paper than in terms of bricks and mortar, at the close of the eighteenth century. Not only was Jefferson a visionary; he had the determination to see his dream become a reality and the strength of purpose to carry through his grandiose scheme. He was seventy-three when the cornerstone on the first pavilion was laid, and impatient with the constant delays attendant on any official undertaking. In order to hasten the work, for instance, he ordered carved capitals from Italy before the expenditure had in fact been sanctioned. He had the satisfaction of living long enough to see the doors of the University opened to students for the first time on March 7, 1825.

The agent or overseer at Monticello, Captain Bacon, recalled that Jefferson, a professional lawyer if an amateur architect, wrote the deed for the purchase of the land himself and lost no time in laying out the ground. Bacon writes:

* Last words of his friend President John Adams, who, in fact, outlived Jefferson by only twelve hours.

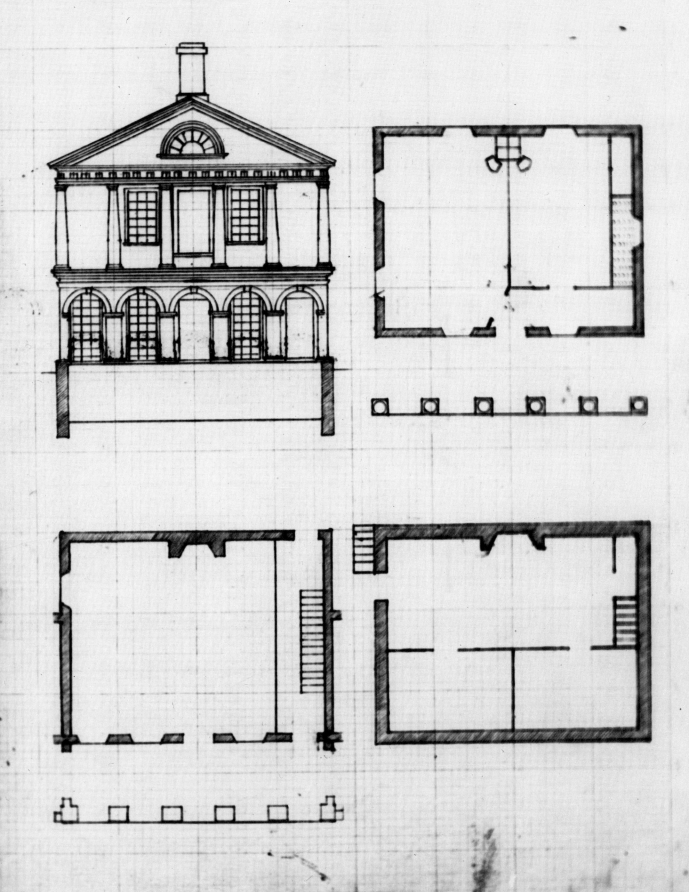

The University, Pavilion VII: The order is the Doric of Palladio, derived from an illustration in Chambray.

The University of Virginia, Pavilion VII: Mr. Jefferson's drawing of the first building of his "academical village." The cornerstone was laid on October 6, 1817. It was in this pavilion that Jefferson used a suggestion by Dr. William Thornton as a basis for his design.

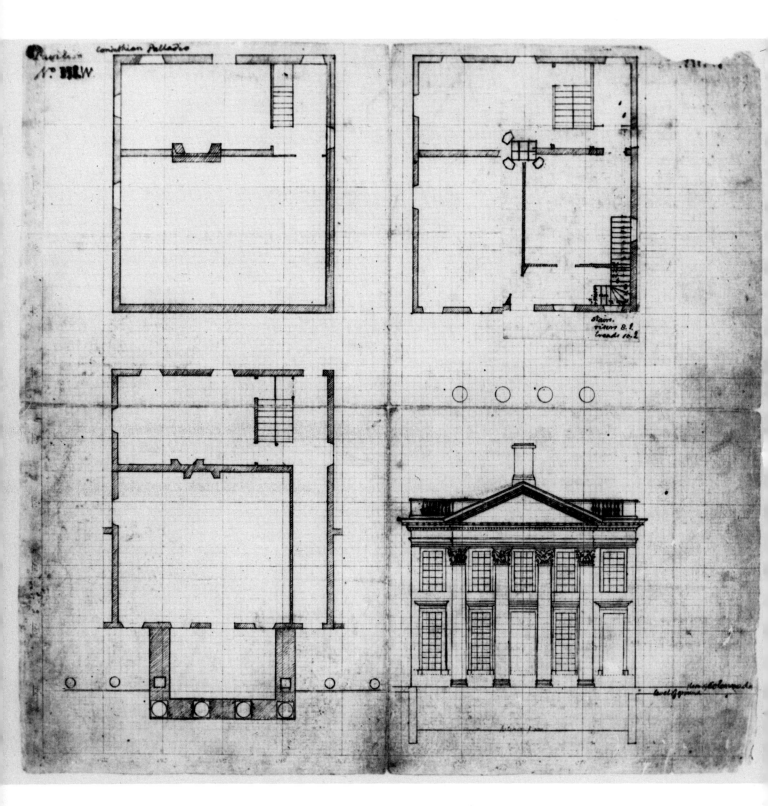

The University, Pavilion III: Mr. Jefferson's drawing,
showing the original parapet, which has been removed.
Here he employed the Corinthian order from Palladio.

The University, Pavilion V: In this building Jefferson used Palladio's Ionic order with modillions. Pavilions III and V were the second and third to be constructed.

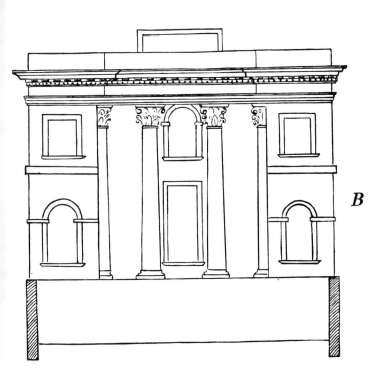

B

The University, Pavilion VIII: Suggested by Latrobe, the order employed here is the Corinthian from the Baths of Diocletian, from Chambray. The parapet has been removed.

The University, Pavilion IX: The entrance motif was a favorite with Ledoux, whose work Jefferson had much admired in France. The Ionic order of the Temple of Fortuna Virilis from Palladio was used here. These first four West Lawn pavilions were completed by the end of September 1821.

The University, Pavilion
I: A detail of the cornice.

The University, Pavilion
I: For this pavilion, completed in 1822, Mr. Jef-
ferson used the Doric
order from the Baths of
Diocletian.

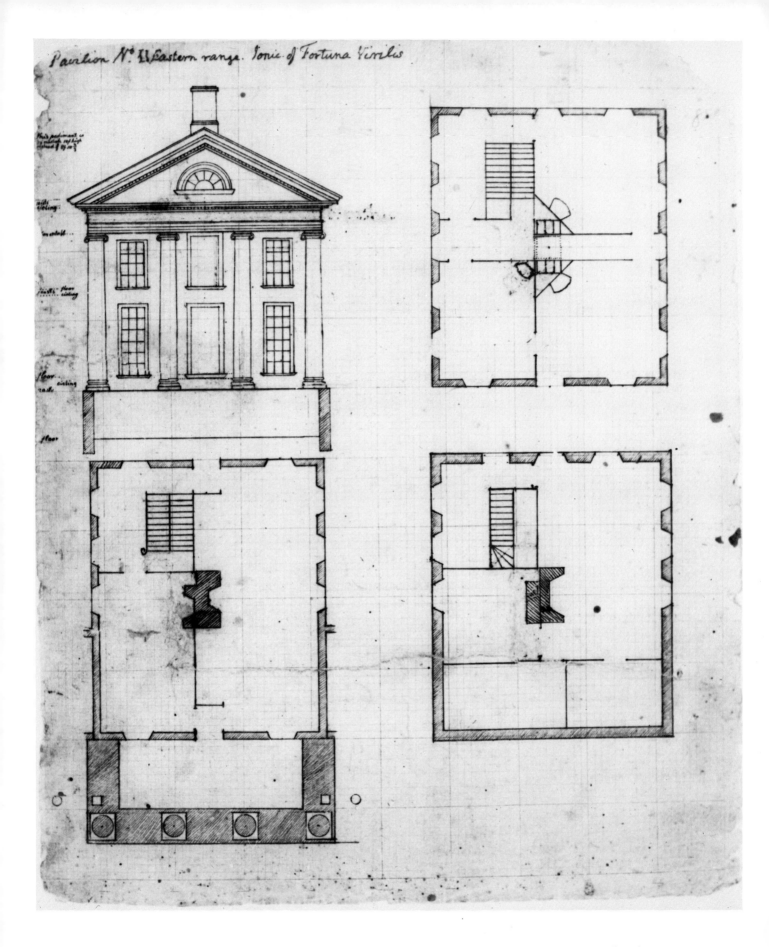

The University, Pavilion II: Mr. Jefferson's drawing, employing the Ionic order from the Temple of Fortuna Virilis, from Palladio. The drawings for the five East Lawn pavilions were done in 1819, in no more than fifteen days. At that time, Thomas Jefferson was seventy-six years of age.

The University, Pavilion IV: The order is the Doric
of Albano, from Chambray. Mr. Jefferson's drawing.

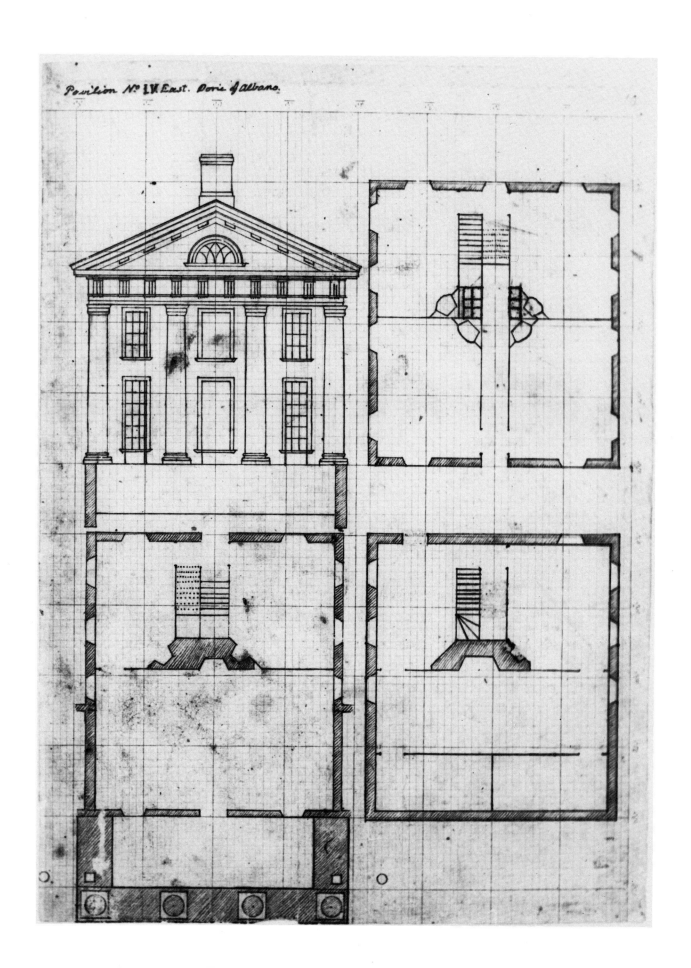

The University, Pavilion X: Mr. Jefferson's drawing, using the Doric order from the Theatre of Marcellus, from Chambray. The parapet, which is no longer extant, was derived from that of the Temple of Nerva Trajan, from Palladio.

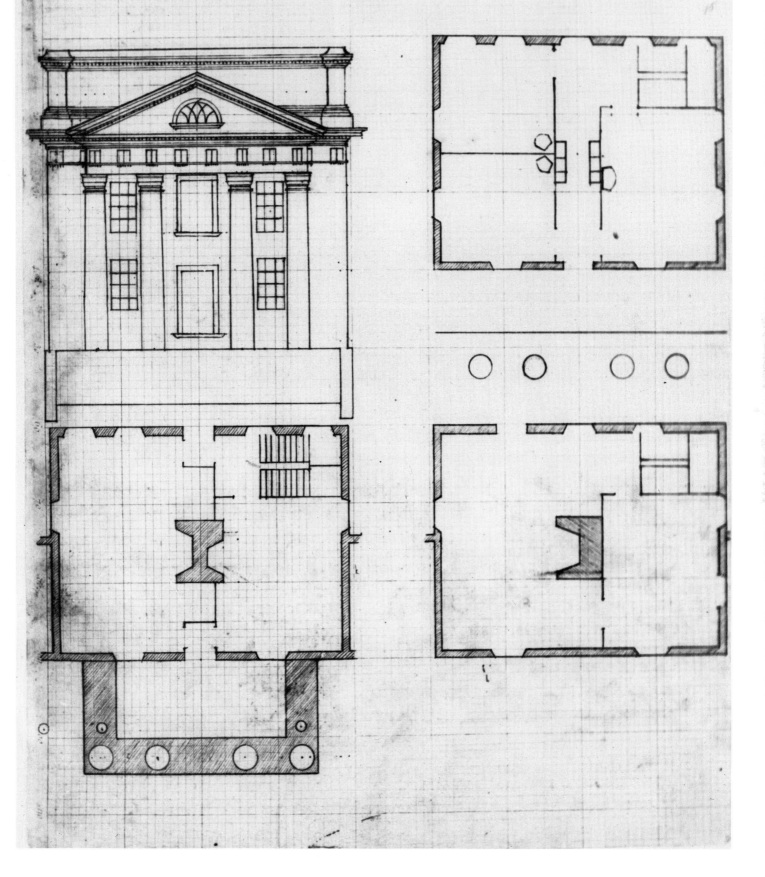

"My next instruction was to get ten able-bodied hands to commence the work. I soon got them, and Mr. Jefferson started from Monticello to lay off the foundations and see the work commenced. An Irishman named Dinsmore* found some shingles and made some pegs, and we all went on to the old field together. Mr. Jefferson looked over the ground some time and then stuck down a peg. He stuck the very first peg in that building, and then directed where to carry the line and I stuck the second. He carried one end of the line, and I the other, in laying off the foundation of the University." Captain Bacon goes on to describe the laying of the foundation stone of what is now Pavilion VII, by President Monroe on October 6, 1817. "After this he rode there from Monticello every day which the University was building, unless the weather was very stormy."

The idea of a model University had been germinating in Jefferson's mind for ten years or more, and the layout was his invention. He had arrived at a solution by 1805, when he wrote to Littleton Tazewell on January 5 that the greatest danger for new colleges "will be their overbuilding, by attempting a large house in the beginning, sufficient to contain the whole institution. Large houses are always ugly, inconvenient, exposed to accident of fire, and bad in cases of infection. A plain small house for the school and lodging of each professor is best, these connected by covered ways out of which the rooms of the students should open would be best. These may then be built only as they shall be wanting. In fact an University should not be an house but a village." His inspiration may have been the illustrations of Palladio, the cloistered colleges in England, or the monasteries he must have seen on his travels in France and Italy, which had covered ways to give protection from the elements.

Jefferson consulted two architects, William Thornton and Benjamin Latrobe, both of whom had been involved in the new Capitol which was building in Washington at the time of his Presidency. In spite of their violent public altercation over that design, he had apparently succeeded in remaining on terms with both of them. Having outlined the general scheme to Thornton, he goes on to write: "Now what we wish, is that these pavilions, as they will show themselves above the dormitories, shall be models of taste and good architecture, and of a variety of appearance, no two alike, so as to serve as specimens for the architectural lecturer. Will you set your imagination to work and sketch some designs for us? No matter how loosely with the pen, without the trouble of referring to scale or rule; for we want nothing but the outline of the architecture. . . . A few sketches such as will not take you a moment will greatly oblige us."

* James Dinsmore, a skilled joiner, was brought from Philadelphia to Monticello in 1798 and worked there on the building until 1808.

"The whole of these arranged around an open square of grass and trees would make it, what it should be in fact, an academical village."

OVERLEAF: "View of the University of Virginia, Charlottesville, and Monticello, from Lewis Mountain," a lithograph published by C. Bohn in 1856.

Thornton obliged with two sketches and some ideas, but Jefferson was evidently not satisfied with them, as he is soon writing along the same lines to Latrobe. Latrobe replies: "I have long considered the common plan of a college as most radically defective.—In your design the principal evils of the usual *barrack* arrangement appear to be avoided." And later: "I have found so much pleasure in studying the plan of your college. . . ." It was Latrobe who suggested the dominant central feature, a building "which ought to exhibit in mass and details as perfect a specimen of good architectural taste as can be devised." The idea of the Rotunda was born. Without it the dramatic impact of the Lawn would be lost. Jefferson placed the Rotunda at the summit, looking down the orderly rows of dazzling white pillars to the empty plain beyond—empty no longer. One end of the quadrangle was left open; Jefferson proposed an arboretum at the lower end of the Lawn, planted in exotic trees and shrubs, as a pleasure ground for the enjoyment of students and faculty. Unfortunately, however, later buildings have closed the quadrangle.

The Rotunda was designed as a library, the heart of any university, and it was typical of the rationalist in Jefferson to give it pride of place over the "room for religious worship" that was only a fraction of its size. This concept of a temple of learning was a departure from the traditional custom whereby the principal building in a university was invariably the chapel. The Rotunda was surmounted by a vast gilded weather vane in the shape of a quill pen,* which was later taken down when some dauntless student attached the Confederate flag to it. The Visionary architect Jean-Jacques Lequeu (1757–1825) designed a mausoleum for Voltaire surmounted by a globe and a quill pen resembling a weather vane, suggesting the world-wide influence of Voltaire's pen. Jefferson proposed that the concave ceiling of the Rotunda's dome be painted sky-blue and adorned with the constellations; probably after the design of Etienne-Louis Boullée (1728–1799), another Visionary architect, who designed the interior of an imaginary cenotaph, dedicated to his hero Isaac Newton, in the form of an immense sphere, the upper half or dome painted with the moon and stars. Jefferson was obviously familiar with the work of the Visionaries. He even designed a boom whereby the unfortunate draftsman could be suspended in mid-air while fixing the gilt stars in their rightful positions.

* This was in fact added to a cupola which was not in Jefferson's design but which had been necessitated by leaks in the skylight. The quill pen was 8 or 10 feet long and was seen and described in 1858 by Captain John W. Payne of Amherst, Virginia, an alumnus.

Pavilion VII, the first to be constructed—and
behind the colonnades, rooms for students.

The design of the Rotunda was taken from the Pantheon in Rome reduced to half-scale, the diameter and height being 77 feet. The curve of the dome, if carried on, would have come full circle at basement level. The basement contained three oval rooms, and on the main floor there were also three oval rooms, to be used for religious worship and (in Jefferson's words) "by schools of instruction in drawing, music, or any other of the innocent and ornamental accomplishments in life. . . ." The vast circular room above the main floor was the library, the bookshelves running between the walls and the twin columns of the Composite order. These in turn gave support to an upper gallery, which provided more space for books. The library must have been spectacular as built, lighted by its fourteen windows and the skylight. The working tables and benches were made on a curve, and small "rooms" for study were provided between the bookshelves.

The Rotunda was first used as a banquet hall to honor the Marquis de Lafayette during the course of his triumphal tour of the country in 1824, although it was not quite finished at that date. Jefferson's patience was running out; in December of that year he writes: "When shall we get our roses for the Rotunda? The whole scaffolding of the building is obliged to be kept standing only to enable the workmen to put up these small ornaments." There was difficulty over customs imposts also, on the carved stone capitals from Italy that "are so heavy that 2 different ships at Leghorn refused to take them." After much correspondence, continuing until the year of his death, the duty was remitted; Jefferson was thus enabled to order (on June 4, 1826) the Simon Willard turret clock and the bell for the Rotunda. Willard stated that Jefferson's plans and specifications were the only ones he ever received that were properly worked out. So accurate and so clearly drawn were they that, when he came to install the clock, everything fitted to the sixteenth of an inch.

The University of Virginia: It is believed that this plan was drawn by Jefferson and shaded by Cornelia Randolph. It shows the original roof forms. The Rotunda is here omitted, though it was drawn after Latrobe's suggestion for the dominant central feature.

The University, East Lawn: ". . . joining these lodges by barracks for a certain portion of the students, opening into a covered way to give a dry communication between all the schools."

The University, East Range: Mr. Jefferson's drawing of the center hotel was made about May 1820; it shows the original flat roof and "Chinese railing."

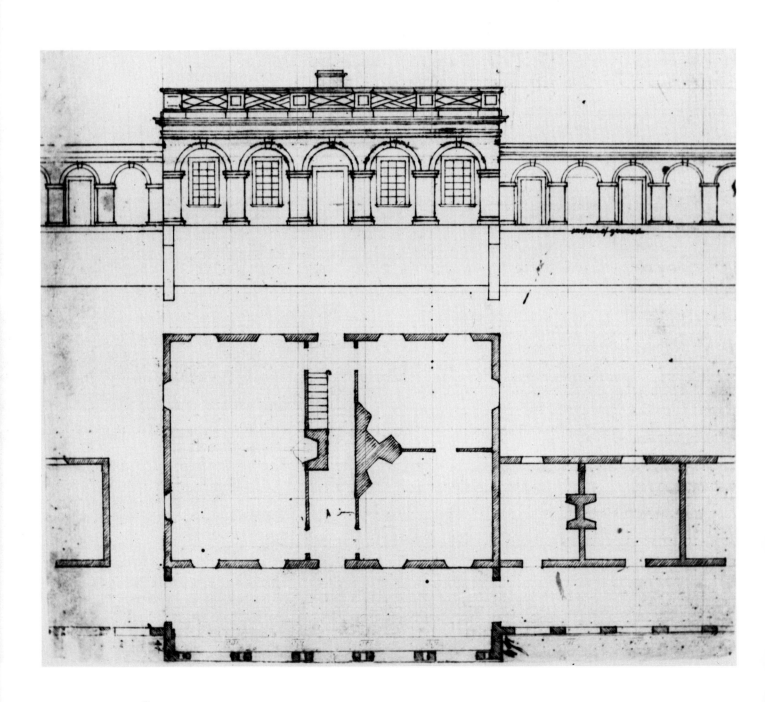

The University, East Range: The northeast hotel, hotel "A" on Cornelia Randolph's perspective, originally had a flat roof and "Chinese railing" similar to that of the center hotel.

The University: This view from the East Range to the back of East Lawn shows the contour of the land which made it necessary for Jefferson to exchange his original three-sided square for the present oblong shape.

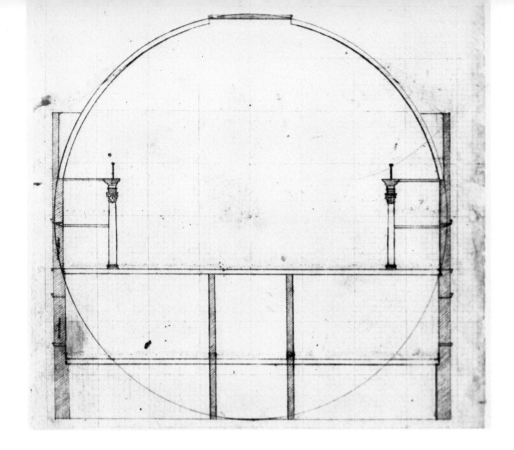

The University, the Rotunda: The section as drawn by
Mr. Jefferson. He found, in Leoni's 1721 edition of
Palladio, eleven plates from which to inform himself
about the Pantheon.

In 1851 it was decided to add an annex to the north side of the Rotunda. The
architect chosen was Robert Mills, the Charleston architect who had been a
protégé of Jefferson and who designed the first and most distinguished of all the
monuments to George Washington, in the heart of the city of Baltimore. The
new addition caught fire in 1895, and the fire spread to the Rotunda, causing
its destruction. Unfortunately it was not resurrected according to Jefferson's
plan. Against the wishes of the entire faculty, a new Rotunda was designed by
the eminent architect Stanford White, differing from the original internally
and adding a north portico with flanking wings which match the Jefferson
wings on the south. Professor Frederick D. Nichols, who directed the restoration of the pavilions, hotels, and dormitories, has documented the Rotunda's
history and will now serve as adviser for its restoration. In 1972 grants were
made by the Cary D. Langhorne Trust and H.U.D. for this purpose. This will
be the first phase of the total restoration of Jefferson's neoclassical building,
being concerned mainly with the interior and the dome. The main-floor oval
rooms will be used by the university president and the Board of Visitors, and
the dome room will become a visitors' center, a museum of university history,
and a place for social occasions; the Rotunda will once again become the center
of the university's life.

The University, the Rotunda: Mr. Jefferson's drawings for the Rotunda may be dated before March 29,
1821, when a careful estimate was made of its cost.

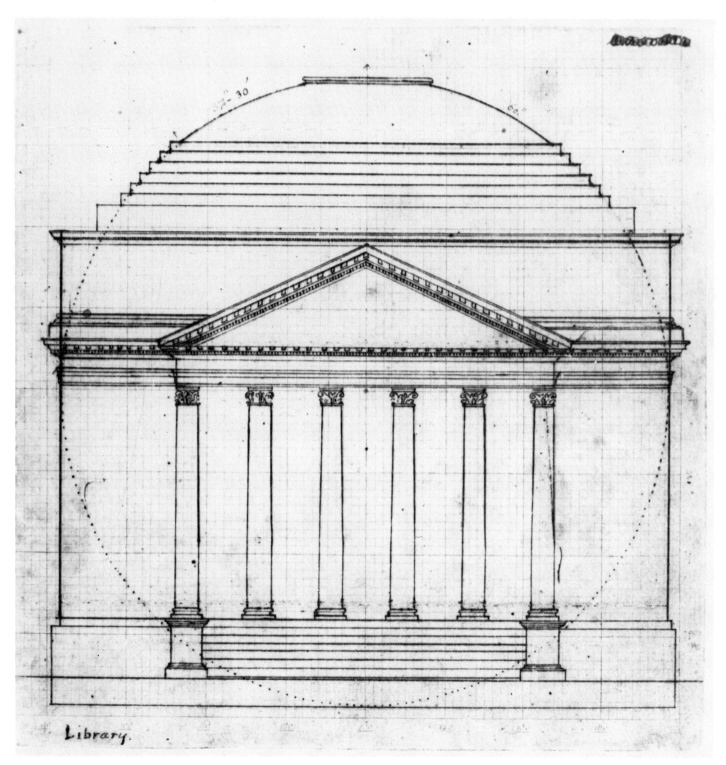

Library.

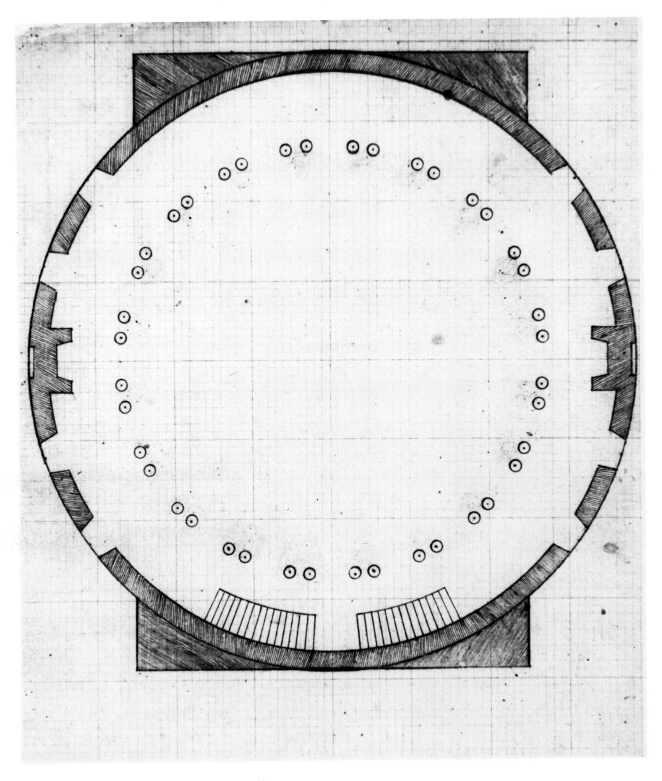

The University, the Rotunda: The Jefferson drawing of the library floor, which is also to be restored. This and the following drawing were on the same sheet; Jefferson's specifications are on the back.

The University, the Rotunda: Thomas Jefferson's drawing of the first floor, which is now to be restored to its original plan; though the rooms will no longer be used for "drawing, music, examinations and other accessory purposes."

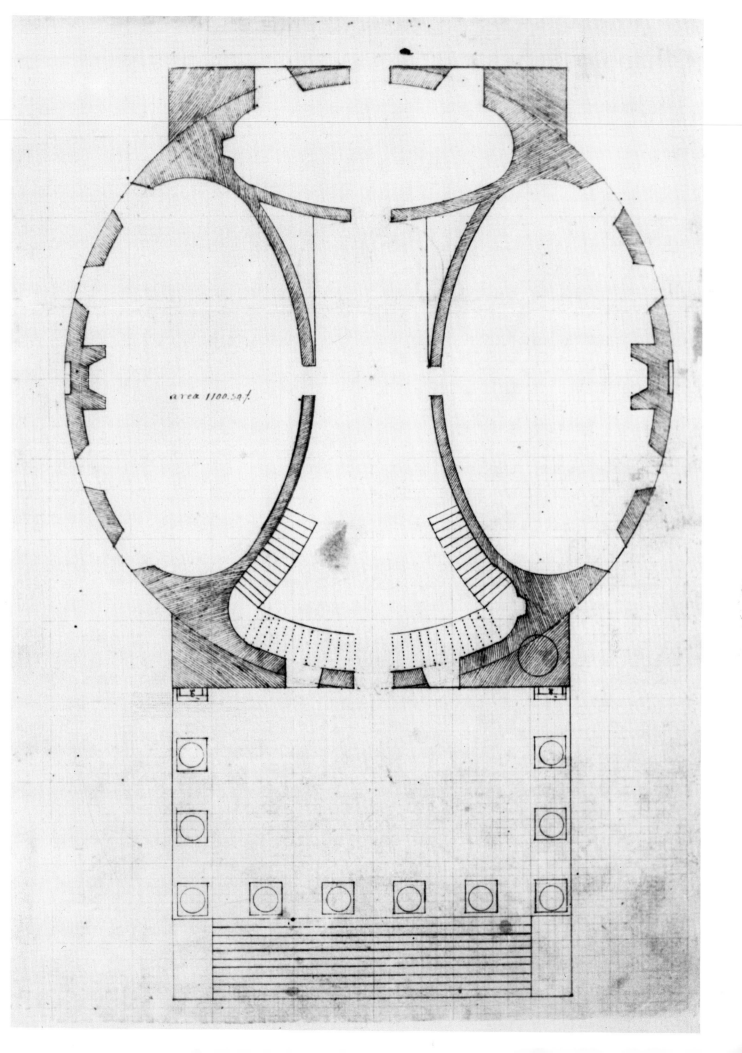

area 1100. sq f.

OPPOSITE:

The University: Thought to be by Jefferson's granddaughter Cornelia, this drawing shows his original conception of the University as viewed from the proposed arboretum.

The University, the Rotunda: This drawing by Calder Loth is a conjectural view of the north front as it was built. Mr. Jefferson's drawings for the Rotunda show no steps to the north door, but the study for the 1822 Maverick plan shows twin flights alongside the base of the building.

The University, the Rotunda: This little-known drawing by Thomas Jefferson for the turret clock hangs in the Willard Homestead in Grafton, Massachusetts. It is one of the last drawings he ever made. Simon Willard, who also made the clock for the United States Senate Chamber, had met Jefferson and visited him at Monticello. The clock was destroyed in the Rotunda fire, but the bell survives and is still on display in the Rotunda.

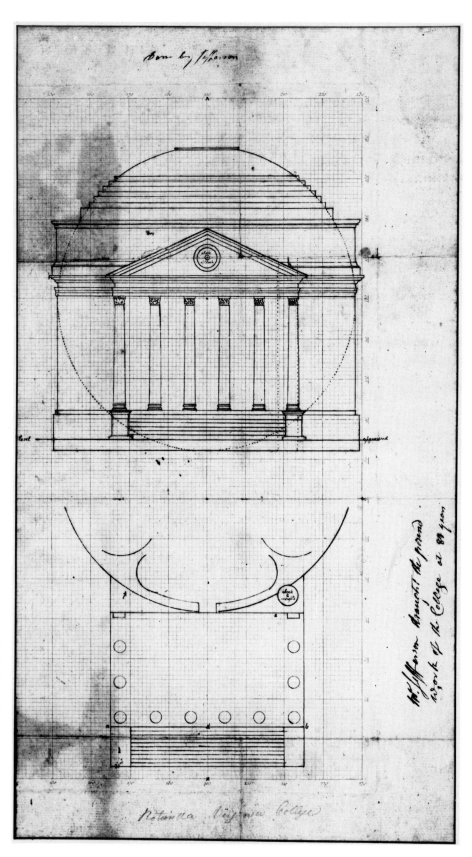

135

EXPLANATIONS,

OF THE GROUND PLAN OF THE UNIVERSITY OF VIRGINIA.

Nos. I, II, III. IV, V, VI, VII, VIII, IX, X, are PAVILIONS, of two stories each, for the residence of the Professors separately, with each a lecturing room, and generally four rooms of accommodation for the family—a back yard and garden. The offices are below.

The small apartments numbered 1, to 55. filling the intervals between the Pavilions, are DORMITORIES of a single story, for two students each ; all opening into a colonnade, along the whole range of 600 feet in length. These Dormitories have a flat roof, in the level of the upper floor of the Pavilions, which, through the Porticos, gives a private walk and communication to the families inhabiting the Pavilions.

A, B, C, D, E, F, are HOTELS, to be let to housekeepers for dieting the students. The small intervening apartments, numbered 1 to 56, are DORMITORIES, as those of the two middle rows, all opening into arcades, continued along the whole range, 600 feet in length each, These Hotels have their offices below, with each a back-yard and garden, separated by cross-streets of communication with the Pavilions.

The ground between the two middle rows, in front and back of the ROTUNDA, is an open lawn looking S. S. E. 200 feet wide, and at present 900 feet in length, left open at one end for a continuation of the buildings indefinitely.

The ROTUNDA, filling up the Northernmost end of the ground is 77 feet in diameter, and in height, crowned by a Dome of 120 deg. of the sphere. The lower floor has large rooms for religious worship, for public examinations, and other associated purposes. The upper floor is a single room for a Library, canopied by the Dome and it's sky-light.

The Rotunda is connected with the two rows of Pavilions by a TERRAS on each side of the height of its Basement, and breadth of the flank of it's Portico; below the Terras is a space for gymnastick exercises, and a covered way uniting those of the two colonnades, and affording a sheltered passage round three sides of the lawn, 1400 feet in extent.

Within the back-yards are cisterns of fountain water, brought in pipes from a neighbouring mountain.

☞ *Plans of the University of Virginia. can be had by applying to the Proctor. at 50 cents each, and the Report of the Commissioners at 12 1-2 cents.*

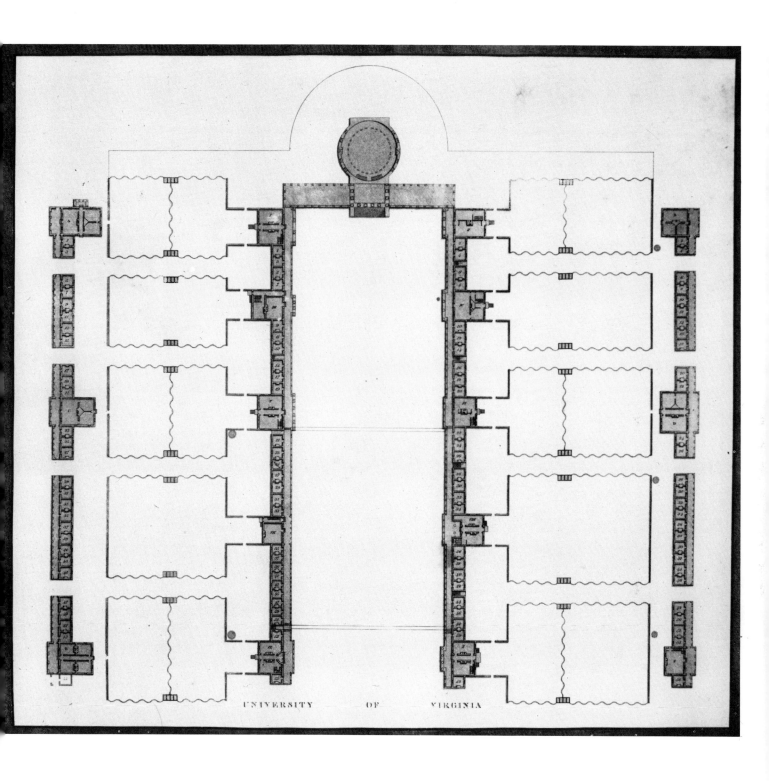

UNIVERSITY   OF   VIRGINIA

The University, the Maverick Engraving: This second
edition of the Maverick plan was delivered March 3,
1825. It was executed by Peter Maverick of New York,
based on a drawing by Mr. Jefferson.

The University: A detail from the 1856 "View from
Lewis Mountain," which appears in color on pages 122
and 123. Pavilion III still retains its parapet and hotel
"A" its "Chinese railing." Hotels "B" and "D," on the
West Range, also resemble their original drawings
more closely.

Jefferson originally decreed that the two enfilades of student rooms would have flat roofs, so that the faculty who lived on the upper floors of the pavilions could visit one another without coming down to the level of the students—another idea that would have appealed to the Visionary architects. Both Thornton and Latrobe advised against this, and in the event they were proved right; the flat roofs gave trouble and in time were replaced with hipped roofs of conventional design.

Behind the pavilions he provided for large gardens, separated by serpentine walls, built partly for economy, as they are strong enough to stand when only one brick in thickness, but mainly to throw exciting shadows on the pathways and impart a ripple of movement and life to the gardens themselves. The Garden Club of Virginia has recently restored the walls to their former beauty.

The University: The photograph shows the interior of the library before the fire of 1895. This room, which occupies the top storey of the Rotunda, is where the banquet in honor of General Lafayette was held. Omitted in Stanford White's reconstruction, it is now being restored.

The University: The fire on Sunday, October 24, 1895, which destroyed the Rotunda.

The University, a rosette: One of the applied rosettes surviving from the original Carrara marble capitals.

The University, an unfinished capital: This decorative capital, never completed or installed, is an example of Jefferson's effort to use capitals cut from native stone. He reports that "on trial the stone we had counted on in the neighborhood of the University was found totally unsusceptible of delicate work. . . ."

The University, an Italian capital: After the failure with native stone, Jefferson ordered marble capitals from Italy. They arrived in 1825 and were placed on the south portico of the Rotunda. The example shown, salvaged from the fire, is now a garden ornament. Unexpectedly, the University was called upon to pay a heavy duty on these imported bits of stonework: having paid it, Jefferson felt it impossible to order the clock and bell for the Rotunda. It was not until Congress had passed a special bill remitting the duty that Jefferson felt enabled to place his order with Simon Willard.

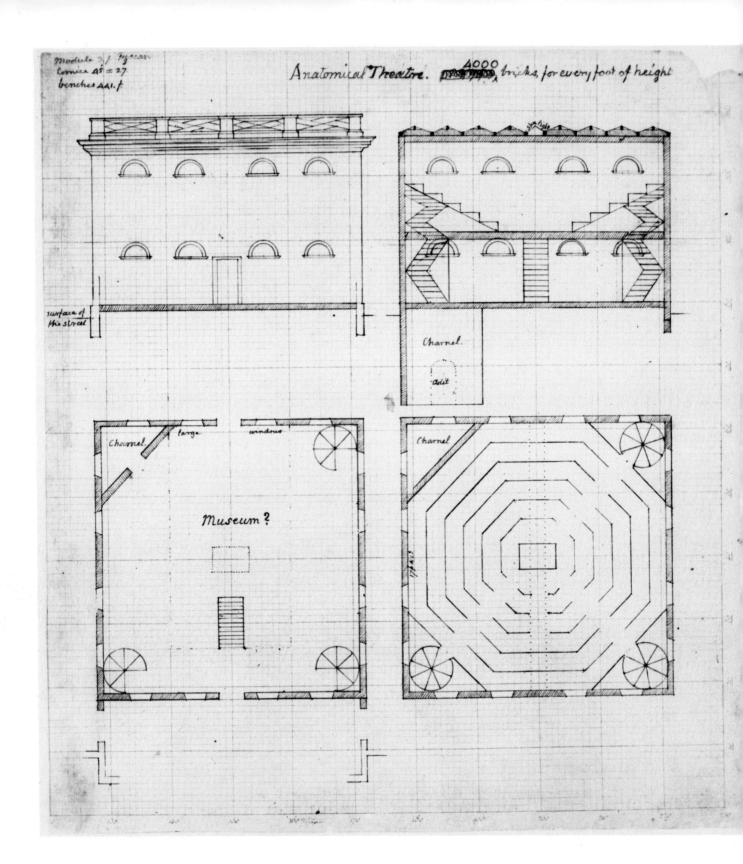

The University, the anatomical theater: Mr. Jefferson's drawing for the only one of his buildings at the University which has not survived. It was one of the last of the original buildings to be started, in 1826, and was unfinished at the time of his death. A skylight and high windows provided light for the operating theater.

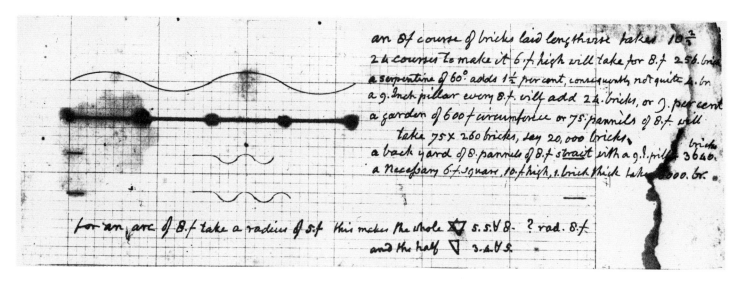

an 8f course of bricks laid lengthwise takes 10½
24 courses to make it 6 f high will take for 8.f 256. brick
a serpentine of 60° adds 1½ per cent, consequently not quite 4. br
a 9. inch pillar every 8.f will add 24. bricks, or 9. per cent
a garden of 600 f circumference or 75. pannels of 8.f will
        take 75 x 260 bricks, say 20,000 bricks
a back yard of 8. pannels of 8.f strait with a 9.I. pillar 3640. bricks
a Necessary 6.f square, 10.f high, 1. brick thick takes 2000. br.

for an arc of 8.f take a radius of 5.f this makes the whole ☒ 5.5.∀8. ? rad. 8.f
                                          and the half ∇ 3.4.∀s.

The University: This drawing of Mr. Jefferson's shows
how to build both straight and serpentine walls.
Many examples of this form are to be found in England, where he probably saw them while touring that
country with his friend John Adams.

The University: Restored walls follow the layout shown on the Maverick plan.

THE UNIVERS

The University, from the east: An engraving executed
by "Porte Crayon" (David Hunter Strother), during
the course of a visit to Charlottesville in the autumn of
1853. He later served as a topographer with the Union
Army, and was quartered for a time at Belle Grove.
He felt that the University "has a very pleasing and

OF VIRGINIA.

pretty effect but the buildings are too low and the architecture wants finish. . . ." This is the first print to
show the Annex: the dome has a lantern and weather
vane, but lacks steps at its base. The Annex was designed by Robert Mills, who had worked with Thomas
Jefferson as a student of architecture.

The University: The Lawn.

The University: The Rotunda as it has appeared since Stanford White's reconstruction of 1900.

146

The University: "Withdrawn by age from all other public services and attentions to public things, I am closing the last scenes of life by fashioning and fostering an establishment for the instruction of those who are to come after us. I hope its influence on their virtue, freedom, fame and happiness, will be salutary

and permanent. The form and distributions of its structure are original and unique, the architecture chaste and classical, and the whole well worthy of attracting the curiosity of a visit."

Thomas Jefferson to Judge Augustus B. Woodward, April 3, 1825.

Many had to be rebuilt, as in more Philistine days some had fallen, and even given way to internal roadways. The "necessary houses" and cisterns, perilously close to one another, can be seen in the gardens on the engraved plan by Maverick. Beyond the gardens the plan shows two more rows of student rooms, punctuated by three "Hotels" where meals were provided, and linked by an arcaded covered way. This plan was commissioned by Jefferson for use as a prospectus for the University, accompanied by the Explanations reproduced on page 136.

Jefferson insisted that his University could not have been built more economically than it was, and here the practical side of his nature comes face to face with the visionary. Equal accommodation to that provided could of course have been built for less, but at the cost of beauty—indeed, as much could be said of any great cathedral in Europe. He writes to Madison from France in 1785, referring to architecture: "It is an enthusiasm of which I am not ashamed, as its object is to improve the taste of my countrymen, to increase their reputation, to reconcile them to the respect of the world and procure them its praise." His wish was to elevate the mind through beautiful buildings and gardens elegantly spaced, framed by the mountains on the distant horizon. He succeeded in more than that: his creation excited great interest in Europe at the time, as is evident from the quantity of foreign engravings that were made of it. Ever since, it has been a source of wonder and delight not only to those fortunate enough to attend the University, but to the thousands who make pilgrimage to visit it every year.

"Folly": An original serpentine wall at "Folly," near Staunton, designed by Jefferson for his friend Joseph Smith. The serpentine walls at "Folly" antedate those at the University by two years.

OAK HILL

LEESBURG, VIRGINIA

MR. AND MRS. JOSEPH PRENDERGAST

Oak Hill was built in 1819 for James Monroe, the fifth President of the United States, during his first term in office. The principal feature of the house is the gigantic portico which looks out across the formal terraced garden to the great expanse beyond. It has five columns rather than the usual four, and these are thirty feet in height; the portico was in fact very much grander in scale than the house to which it was attached. The balance has now been redressed; in 1920 the house was extended to either side, with the result that it is no longer dwarfed by the splendid portico.

Jefferson, as an old friend of the Monroes, is thought to have been involved in the design. In June 1820 he writes: "Th. J. to the President: Instead of the unintelligible sketch I gave you the other day, I send it drawn more at large. Mrs. Monroe and yourself may take some hints from it for a better plan of your own. This supposes 10. f. in front, and 8. f in flank added to your villa. a flat of 12. f. square is formed at the top, to make your present rafters answer, and to lighten the appearance of the roof. Affectionate and respectful salutations." The letter shows that Jefferson was offering advice to the Monroes on architectural matters at the time they were occupied with the building of Oak Hill.

It has often been suggested that James Hoban was the principal architect of the house, but in the absence of documentary proof, on stylistic grounds this seems unlikely. Kimball had evidently not seen the letter from Jefferson to Monroe quoted above and did not believe that Jefferson was involved with the design of Oak Hill. He does mention a letter from Monroe to Jefferson as early as 1786, requesting a plan for a house to be built near Richmond. He goes on to quote Major R. W. M. Noland as stating categorically that "the Oak Hill house was planned by Mr. Monroe, but the building superintended by Mr. Wil-

Oak Hill: A photograph taken before the wings were enlarged in the 1920s.

Oak Hill: To the south, the great house overlooks an impressive formal garden and the countryside beyond it. The five columns of the portico allow unobstructed views from the windows in the rooms behind.

liam Benton, an Englishman, who occupied the mixed relation to Mr. Monroe of steward, counselor and friend." Judging by old photographs, the original

Oak Hill would appear to have been built by a builder or master mason, just such a man as Benton. Work was started in 1819. Jefferson's letter of 1820 indicates that he was anxious to help "improve the design." The following letter from Jefferson to Latrobe (August 3, 1817) adds further credence to the theory that the portico may have been his invention: "The pavilion now begun is to be a regular Doric above with a portico of 5 columns (supported by the arches below) and a pediment of the whole breadth of the front. The columns 16 I. diam. The dormitories will be covered flat, as the offices of the President's house at Washington was, and will furnish a fine walk from the chambers of the professors." The letter refers to a pavilion at the University for which the design was subsequently altered. It is important in that it shows that Jefferson had conceived the peculiar idea of a portico with five columns, and that it was in his mind not very long before Oak Hill was built.

Monroe, like Jefferson, could not afford the life of a country gentleman, and by the time he died, on July 4, 1831, his hospitality had ruined him. He was by then considered one of the old school, "polished in manner, who always dressed in a dark blue coat, buff vest, small clothes and top boots." Among the most notable visitors to make the pilgrimage to Oak Hill was the Marquis de Lafayette, who visited Monroe there in 1824 and 1825 and presented him with the elaborate marble mantels that may still be seen in the two main drawing rooms. Monroe had earned the gratitude of the marquis while serving as Minister in Paris shortly after the French Revolution. It was thanks to his personal intervention that Madame de Lafayette was rescued from the guillotine—two mantels for one wife.

Monroe's grandson, Samuel L. Gouverneur, Jr., sold Oak Hill in 1852 to Colonel John Fairfax, who owned it through the time of the Civil War and sold it in 1870 to a Dr. Quimby. In 1877 Colonel Fairfax's son Henry bought the property back into that family, and it remained in their hands until 1920. The next owner was Frank C. Littleton, who, with the help of Mr. Henry Whitfield the architect, lengthened the house by about fifteen feet at either side and added the two end porticos.

The present owner and her first husband, the late Thomas DeLashmutt, purchased the estate in 1948 and have done much to improve both house and grounds. The brickwork, which had been painted many times over the years, was uncovered, and the gardens have been brought back to life. The sandy gravel drive is flanked by enormous trees, and great mounds of dark green box herald the approach to the house. Over the years, Mrs. Prendergast has collected pictures and furniture that have historic associations and are well suited to the house in which the Monroe Doctrine was conceived.

VANISHED PUBLIC BUILDINGS

CHRIST CHURCH, CHARLOTTESVILLE

During the years he was occupied with the design and construction of the University, Jefferson furnished plans for a church and two courthouses, which were all built or begun during his lifetime, but which have all since disappeared. Christ Church in Charlottesville was built in 1824; in the manner typical of eighteenth-century classical churches, it resembled a light, airy assembly room. There was a gallery supported on clustered columns with carved capitals, which, judging by a rather faded photograph, appear to have been Corinthian. A handsome wooden balustrade separated the congregation from the altar, which was set back into a niche formed beneath a broad classical entablature. The Gothic texts above the altar were presumably a concession to Victorian taste. Bishop Meade wrote of it: "The plan . . . though far from being the best, is much better for the purposes of worship and preaching than most of those which now come from the hands of ecclesiological architects." The church was pulled down in 1895 and replaced by the "Olde English" Christ Church, considered to be a fine example of Victorian Gothic gloom.

THE BOTETOURT COUNTY COURTHOUSE

The drawings for the courthouse designed by Jefferson at Fincastle in Botetourt County have not survived. Evidence that he designed it lies in a letter

Christ Church: A classical design, Jefferson's Christ
Church was based on Chalgrin's St. Philippe du Roule,
which stood a few blocks from Jefferson's Paris house.

from Jefferson to General James Breckenridge, written in 1818, which refers
to the new building. He wrote: "You have had a right to suppose me very un-
mindful of my promise to furnish you with drawings for your Courthouse. Yet
the fact is not so, a few days after I parted with you, the use of the waters of
the warm spring began to affect me unfavorably . . . by working at your drawings a little every day, I have been able to compleat, and now to forward them
by mail with the explanations accompanying them, I hope your workman will
sufficiently understand them." (Jefferson Papers, Library of Congress). The
county records show that General Breckenridge supervised the construction of
the courthouse, which had the inevitable portico, wings on either side, and a
dome. It burned, and in 1847 was replaced by a new building, probably similar

The Botetourt Courthouse: The successor to Jefferson's courthouse on this site was burned on December 15, 1970. It is being restored again closely following the design of Jefferson's original building.

to the original one, graced with a cupola and spire instead of the dome. This also was destroyed by fire, in 1970, and is to be reconstructed by the local citizens, saddened by the loss of their most distinguished secular building.

The Buckingham County Courthouse

Fate has been equally unkind to the other courthouse that Jefferson designed. In 1821 he sent a set of plans to Charles Yancey, one of the members of the building commission for a new courthouse in Buckingham County. Yancey

The Buckingham Courthouse: Jefferson's building, begun in 1822, was burned in 1869. The structure now standing on the site is similar in size and design to the original.

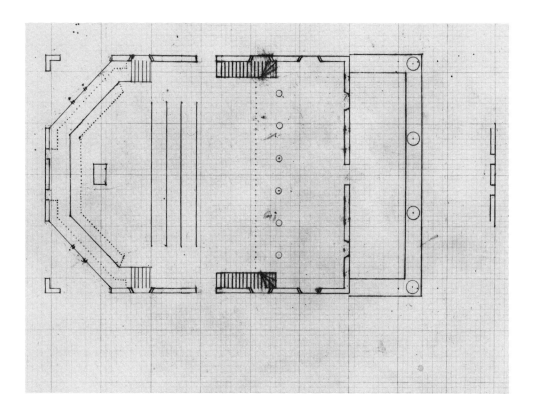

The Buckingham Courthouse: Jefferson's drawing.

had requested plans from his friend Jefferson on the grounds that his architectural knowledge was "a common stock, which we all have a right to draw on." To Yancey's mortification the plans were rejected; the other commissioners wanted to model the new building on the Albemarle Courthouse in Charlottesville. A party traveled to inspect this building, which had been erected in 1803, and consulted the judges and lawyers who practiced there and who were unanimous in their objections to its design. As a consequence of their report, Jefferson's plan was chosen after all, and Yancey's honor was satisfied. The new building was fifty-nine by forty-four feet, fronted by a Tuscan portico, the columns of brick plastered and painted white. The three jury rooms were situated above the judges' bench on the second floor so as to make it difficult for the world outside to communicate with the jurors. There is just the hint of an octagon in the disposition of the benches. The building was in use from 1823 to 1869, when it was destroyed by fire, nearly all the county records going up in smoke at the same time. The present courthouse resembles Jefferson's original plan, which is preserved in the Coolidge Collection together with detailed instructions in his hand.

Frascati: Judge Philip Pendleton Barbour, brother to
the builder of Barboursville, erected Frascati in 1830,
some four years after Jefferson died. The house was at
least in part built by workmen employed in the construction of the University, which goes far to explain
the Jeffersonian influence evident in this fine example
of the Piedmont house of the period.

AMPTHILL

CARTERSVILLE, VIRGINIA

MR. AND MRS. JAMES C. REA., JR.

Ampthill, Cumberland County, stands at the Confluence of the James and Willis Rivers, both of which flow for some distance beside the property. There is an early frame house of 1737, two storeys high, to which a handsome new frontage was added, making an H-shaped plan. Jefferson owned Elk Hill, across the James, and must have been familiar with Ampthill. Fiske Kimball attributed two of Jefferson's drawings in the Coolidge Collection to Ampthill, but it is unlikely that Kimball could have visited the house, as it bears no resemblance to the plans. One of the plans is very curious, showing two lozenge-shaped octagons to either side of a central portico. Kimball based his attribution on an indistinct photograph in R. A. Lancaster's *Historic Virginia Homes and Churches* (1915), in which the house was covered in creeper and practically obscured by bushes and trees. If he had other evidence than this photograph, he made no mention of it.

The present owners of Ampthill and a local historian, Mr. Richard Couture, believe that one of the plans considered by Kimball to correspond with a scheme for the rebuilding of Shadwell might relate to the front part of their house. This was added for Randolph Harrison, formerly of Clifton, to whom Jefferson writes in September 1815: "During a long visit to this place I have had leisure to think of your house. You seemed to require six rooms, neither more nor less, and a good entrance or passage of communication. The enclosed is drawn on that plan. The ground plat is in detail, and exact, the elevation is merely a sketch to give a general idea. The workman, if he is anything of an architect, will be able to draw the particulars. Affectionately yours. . . ."

Ampthill, Cumberland County: Built *ca.* 1830, Ampthill is another example of Jefferson's influence on the local architecture. Retaining the earlier structure, the owner apparently modified its interior and added a wing by adapting a plan of Mr. Jefferson's and including the latest Asher Benjamin motifs.

The new front of Ampthill has eight bays, so that the portico is off-center; otherwise it is a typical Jeffersonian creation. The use of brick, the handsome white portico, and the height of one storey would point to Jefferson, even if the letter quoted above were not adequate proof of his involvement, but it appears that the brick wing was built following Jefferson's death, in the 1830s, after the publishing of Asher Benjamin's *The Practical House Carpenter*. Benjamin's influence may be seen in the mantels, in the trim about doors and windows, and in the importance of the center stair introduced in the older portion of the house. This indicates the use of Jefferson's scheme with the addition of contemporary detailing.

BREMO

Bremo Bluffs, Virginia

Mr. Joseph F. Johnston

Bremo is considered by many to be the supreme example of a country house built under the direct influence of Jefferson's neoclassical revival. Jefferson was a close friend and neighbor to General John Hartwell Cocke, and his ideas and advice were sought, but evidence shows that he did not design the house as it was built. In a letter to the general, Colonel Isaac Coles writes (February 23, 1816): "With Mr. Jefferson I conversed at length on the subject of architecture. Palladio, he said, 'was the Bible.' You should get it and stick close to it. He had sent all books, etc. to Washington or he would have drawn up yr. House for you—it would have been a pleasure to him. . . . Dinsmore who is now in Petersburg he recommends to you as a good and faithful workman." James Dinsmore and John Neilson, "superior house-joiners," appeared at Bremo Recess, a house on the property where the General was living. Dinsmore was already taken up with the University, however, and the credit for the design lies with Neilson, who worked in close collaboration with General Cocke. The cornerstone reads "John Neilson of Albemarle Architect" and was laid in July 1818.

Bremo stands on the crest of a hill, like a great bird with wings outstretched, about to soar over the James River. It consists of a central building, connecting links, and twin pavilions. The long terraces provided by the roofs of the offices, similar to those at Monticello, provide views for miles up and down the valley. The house is one storey on the entrance front, but the façade that faces the river

Bremo: The barn.

is two-storeyed on account of the slope of the land. The ground floor contains the dining room, library, pantry, and storerooms, and the principal living rooms and bedrooms are above. The kitchen, laundry, harness room, schoolroom, and bachelors' quarters are in the wings; other facilities are in separate adjacent buildings. Near the canal stands the splendid Palladian barn, erected prior to the construction of the house; in its clock tower hangs the plantation bell presented to Cocke by the Marquis de Lafayette.

The entrance portico is similar to that at Monticello, although of the simpler Tuscan order rather than the Doric, in deference to General Cocke's austere taste. However, the chief beauty of the building lies in the monumental quality of the wings. The brick wall at the north front of either wing boasts a blind recess, formed like a Palladian window; the south ends terminate in two-storey porches, composed of an arcade supporting a Tuscan order with pediment. Pavilion VII, the first building constructed at the University, the cornerstone of which was laid in 1817, has the same general design. Bremo was completed in 1819/20, and it is safe to assume that the wings were built at the same time as the central block.

General Cocke was, like Jefferson, an amateur architect, and the design of the Fluvanna County Courthouse at Palmyra has been ascribed to him. He built no less than three houses at Bremo, and remodeled one in the Jacobean style to recall the fact that the land had been granted to his family a hundred years earlier. His wife died in 1816, and for a time the general was inconsolable. Out of bereavement, however, he gained a new sense of purpose and started a boys' school where Jefferson's grandsons were educated. Unlike other planters of his day, he refused to grow tobacco, believing it to be harmful to the land as well as to those who used it, and was an advocate of total abstinence from spirits. He built a little classical temple by the canal as a shrine to the "Sons of Temperance," which still stands over a spring below the house, although the coming of the railroad necessitated its removal from the original location.

He was one of Jefferson's close associates in the creation of Central College, the precursor of the University of Virginia, and became a member of the Board of Visitors when the University was chartered in 1819. He gave help and advice to Jefferson in planning and supervising the construction of the University buildings. Although the general preferred a simpler and less expansive architectural style than did Jefferson, he tried even after the latter's death to see that his old friend's ideas were carried out. He lived to the age of eighty-five, long enough to see the University grow to prominence; the creation of Bremo was his major achievement, and the house has remained in the hands of his descendants to the present day. This must be one of the longest land tenures in this country, dating back almost a century before the birth of the United States.

Bremo: The entrance front.

Bremo: The entrance hall.

Bremo: The serving door.

Bremo, the entrance elevation: This was drawn by
Cornelia Randolph as part of a group, including Poplar
Forest and the University, executed as a study in architectural drawing. Because this and the accompanying
plan were known to exist, although both of them
dropped from sight for more than fifty years, it was
for some time believed that Bremo was built to the
design of Mr. Jefferson. Later evidence indicates that
the actual designer was the builder, John Neilson, working closely with General Cocke.

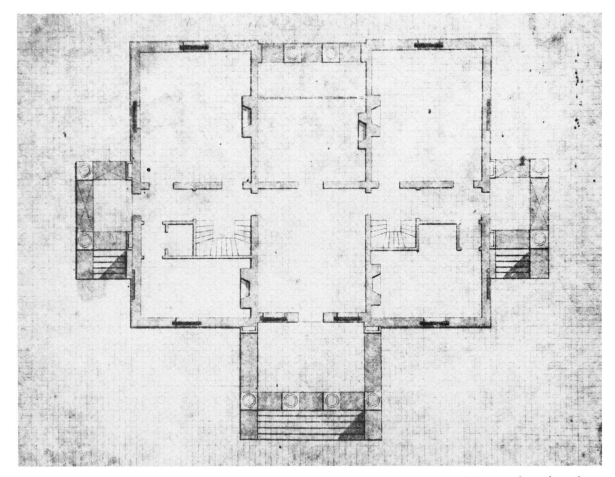

Bremo: The plan by Cornelia Randolph.   OVERLEAF: Bremo: The garden elevation.

Fiske Kimball, in *Thomas Jefferson, Architect* (1916), attributed Bremo to Jefferson on grounds that were subsequently proved false. In 1949, shortly before his death, he wrote: "Of all the houses in the Jeffersonian tradition, not even excepting Monticello, it is Bremo which makes the deepest impression of artistic perfection. Monticello we see drastically remodeled by Jefferson after a change of conception. Bremo has the inevitability of a single ordered creation. Calm, monumental and serene, it commands our emotion as a masterpiece of the art of form."

Acknowledgments

For their generous cooperation in this venture, the authors would like to thank particularly the following people:

The owners of the houses described herein: Mr. and Mrs. Parker Snead of *Edgemont,* Mr. and Mrs. James Watts, Jr., of *Poplar Forest,* Mr. and Mrs. C. Francis Smithers of *Barboursville,* Mr. and Mrs. James C. Rea, Jr., of *Ampthill,* Dr. and Mrs. David R. Hawkins of the *Peter Carr House,* Mr. and Mrs. Joseph Prendergast of *Oak Hill.* Mrs. Marion duPont Scott of *Montpelier,* Mr. Joseph F. Johnston of *Bremo,* Mr. and Mrs. John I. Woodriff of *Frascati,* Dr. and Mrs. W. T. Thompson, Jr., of *Tuckahoe,* and Mr. and Mrs. Joseph S. Cochran, Jr., of *Folly;*

At the Thomas Jefferson Memorial Foundation: The Curator, Mr. James A. Bear, Jr., and Mrs. Leonard Tilman;

At the University of Virginia: Professor Emeritus William B. O'Neal, Professor Frederick Doveton Nichols, and Dean J. Norwood Bosserman of the School of Architecture, Professor Emeritus Bernard Mayo of the History Department, Miss Roy Land, Miss Joan Crane, and Mr. Gregory A. Johnson of the University of Virginia Library, Mr. David M. Skinner of the Department of Graphics, and Mrs. Edwin M. Betts;

At the Virginia State Library: Mrs. Katherine M. Smith, and at the Virginia Historic Landmarks Commission: Mr. Calder Loth.

Acknowledgments are also due to Jacquelin D. J. Sadler, who wrestled with the unenviable task of typing the manuscript. The value of her help and advice on every kind of detail can never be adequately thanked for.

Others whose interest gave great encouragement were Mrs. Iola S. Haverstick, Mr. Milton Grigg, Mrs. Thomas Jefferson Coolidge, Mrs. Melvin Gordon Lowenstein, Mrs. Herbert Forsch, Mrs. Dillman A. Rash, Mr. Wendall Garrett, Miss Sue Ann Sadler, Mr. James F. Waite, Mr. Thomas W. Craven, Mr. Richard Couture, Mr. William T. Stevens, Mr. Roy Wheeler, Dr. Eugene Kusielewicz, Mr. R. F. Loving, Mr. John Evangelisti, Mr. Santino Evangelisti, Miss Conover Hunt, Mr. and Mrs. Cyrus Nathan, and the Editors of *The Iron Worker.*

Gratitude is owed to Peter Fink and Jerome Zerbe, both of whom traveled specially to Virginia in order to take photographs for this book.

The authors will always remember the southern warmth of the hospitality accorded them in Virginia and would like to thank once again Mr. and Mrs. James Lewis, Jr., Mrs. Gilbert Rafferty, Miss Frances Rafferty, Dr. and Mrs. E. D. Vere Nicoll, Mrs. Joseph E. Brown, Mrs. Edwin M. Betts, Mr. and Mrs. George Worthington, IV, Mr. Pierson Scott, Dr. and Mrs. William E. Craddock, Miss Gillian Kyles, Mrs. Robert M. Jeffress, Mr. and Mrs. Samuel S. Moody, Jr., Mr. and Mrs. Willis Van Devanter, and Mr. and Mrs. Nelson McClary.

The Illustrations

For their kind permission to reproduce the illustrations on the pages given, our thanks,to: American Architect and Building News Co., 75; *Antiques* magazine (Arthur Vitols of Helga Studio), 54–55, 60 (left); Bowdoin College Museum of Art, Brunswick, Maine, 53; Gene Campbell, 96 (above, left); Samuel Chamberlain, 69; Christ Church, Charlottesville, Virginia, 156; Colonial Williamsburg Foundation, 8–9, 26; Peter Fink, 19, 30–31, 42–43, 85, 141, (all three photographs), 143 (below), 150, 162–163; Thomas Jefferson Memorial Foundation, 48, 49, 50–51, 59, 60 (above, right, and below, right), 61, 62, 63, 64 (above), 65, 66–67, 68, 70–71, 72, 74; The Library of Congress, Historic American Buildings Survey, 168 (below, right), 170–171.

Also: Nelson McClary, 153; Maryland Historical Society, Baltimore, 38 (above); Massachusetts Historical Society, Boston, 20–21, 23, 29, 39, 90 (below), 106–107, 159; The National Trust for Historic Preservation, L. A. Durnier, 78, 79; New York Public Library, Rare Book Division, Astor, Lenox and Tilden Foundations, the end paper map; David Plowden, 56, 58, 100–101, 115 (above), 121, 124, 129 (below); J. Sadler, 105 (below); Ralph R. Thompson, 91.

And: University of Virginia, Manuscripts Division, 10, 11, 13, 34, 35, 38 (below), 94, 95, 110, 112, 116, 117, 119, 126, 128, 130, 131, 132, 133, 134 (above and below), 136, 142, 144–145, 169 (above and below); University of Virginia, Department of Graphics, 111, 113, 114 (above and below), 115 (below), 118, 122–123, 127, 129 (above), 137, 138, 139, 143 (above), 146, 147, 148–149, 172; Valentine Museum (Cook Collection), Richmond, Virginia, 140; Virginia State Library, Richmond, 14, 15, 28 (above and below), 32, 47, 64 (below), 82, 84, 90 (above), 96 (below, left), 104–105, 105 (above), 152, 157, 158, 160, 166, 168 (above, and below, left).

Finally: The Western Reserve Historical Society, 80; The Willard Homestead, 135; Michiel Wystma, 97; Jerome Zerbe, 88–89, 89 (above and below), 96 (above, right, and below, right), 108, 168 (above).

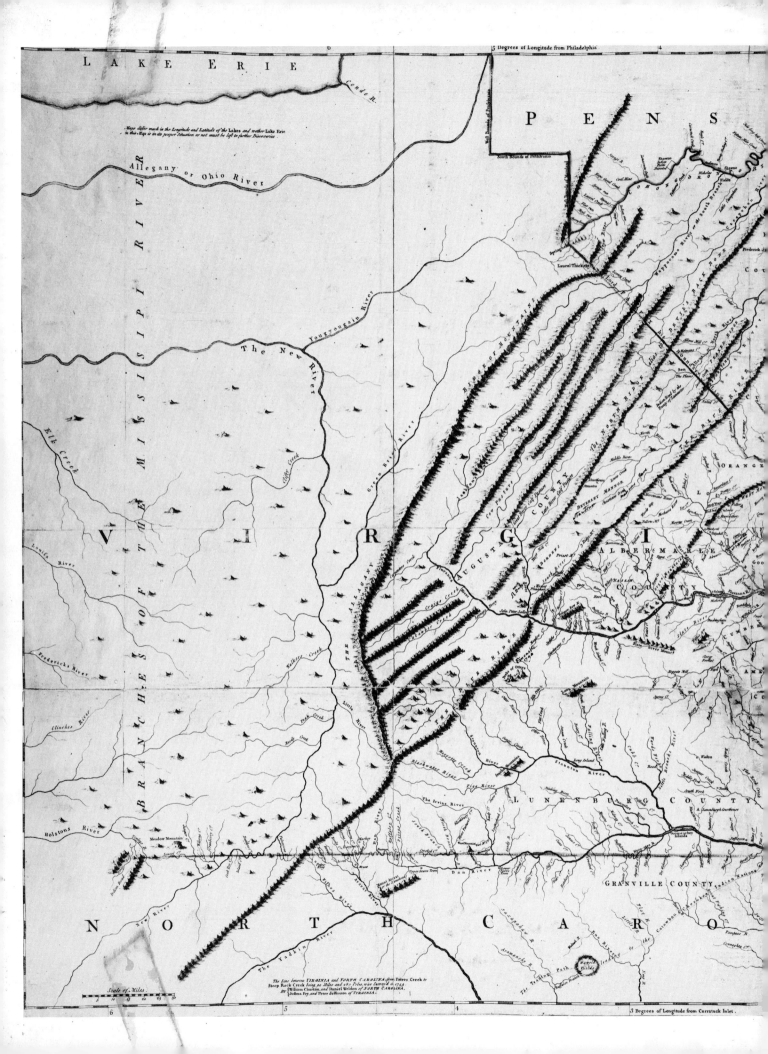